I'll
HAVE
it my
WAY

For thirty years I've worked in a hospital setting, including the first twenty as a social worker in ICU (intensive care unit). In that time, I've counseled hundreds of patients and their families as they struggled with decisions concerning their loved one's serious illness or end-of-life care without the benefit of previous planning and communication. Hattie Bryant's own experience as an advocate for her dying mother affords her the opportunity to credibly and passionately present the case for personal responsibility in the healthcare and end-of-life decisions that await us all. Using the valuable thought processes and exercises in this book to guide our personal plans, we can remove the burden of difficult decision-making from our loved ones and focus instead on living our lives fully to the end.

– Elizabeth Chaitin, DHCE, MA, MSW
    Director of Quality and Ethics
    University of Pittsburgh Medical Center Palliative
        and Supportive Institute

Finding a way to motivate people like us to think about the choices and decisions that need to be made when we are confronted with a serious life-threatening illness has always been difficult, because it raises the possibility or even probability of dying and death. We would prefer not to think about it, much less talk about it with family, friends and our physicians. This is painful, emotional stuff.

Knowledge is power. Knowing the flaws and gaps in care that currently exist in modern medical care for the chronically ill, the fragile elderly, and those with incurable disease helps us develop a plan to have a voice in the care we receive in the future, when it's our turn. It is important to make a plan now, before we get too ill to make good decisions.

Hattie Bryant, determined to help others avoid the difficulties she and her mother endured as her mother died, has used her communication and organization skills to provide the steps to guide you in this process. An experienced educator, she has had the advice and counsel of many national experts in palliative care, geriatrics, oncology, bioethics, psychology and spirituality in writing this book for you. Have it your way.

– John P. (Jack) McNulty, MD, FACP, FAAHPM
  Tulane Medical School, Class of 1951

We live in a death-denying society. No one wants to talk or think about, and certainly not make plans for it. So it makes sense that when it is our turn to die (and we all have an appointment), we are many times not prepared. Hattie Bryant candidly and compellingly confronts this issue in *I'll Have it My Way.* While it is vital for people to think about and make plans for what they want *before* they have been diagnosed with a serious, possibly life-threatening illness, human nature all too often works against our better self. The trend of adult children also caring for aging parents compounds the issue, but Hattie provides a powerful and encouraging companion guide for decision-making that will equip the reader with both a sense of freedom and great peace, too.

– Pam Malloy, RN, MN, FPCN
  Director and Co-Investigator of the ELNEC Project- End
    of Life Nursing Education Consortium
  American Association of Colleges of Nursing (AACN)

bright sky press
HOUSTON, TEXAS

2365 Rice Blvd., Suite 202
Houston, Texas 77005

10   9   8   7   6   5   4   3   2   1

Library of Congress Cataloging-in-Publication Data

Bryant, Hattie.
I'll have it my way / Hattie Bryant.
     pages cm
Includes bibliographical references.
ISBN 978-1-942945-00-0 (alk. paper)
1. Right to die. 2. Advance directives (Medical care) I. Title.
II. Title: I will have it my way.

R726.B79 2015
179.7--dc23   2015032295

Editorial Direction: Lucy Herring Chambers
Managing Editor: Lauren Adams
Designer: Marla Y. Garcia

Printed in Canada through Friesens

I'll HAVE *it my* WAY

Taking Control *of* End-*of*-Life Decisions

Hattie Bryant

bright sky press

HOUSTON, TEXAS

THIS BOOK IS DEDICATED TO THE
PALLIATIVE MEDICINE TEAMS–PHYSICIANS,
NURSES, CHAPLAINS, PSYCHOLOGISTS,
SOCIAL WORKERS, PHARMACISTS,
VOLUNTEERS, DIETITIANS AND COUNSELORS–
WHO TRULY WANT US TO LIVE FULLY
ALL THE WAY TO THE END.

AND TO MY MOM AND DAD WHO
SHOWED ME THE WAY.

OUR HEALTH is our personal responsibility. I learned this in 1990 while watching my mom die. She was passive in life—sweet, soft-spoken and deferred first to her bossy mother then to my bossy dad. It was my dad who had the living wills done for the two of them. I would have thought that when she lost all cognitive functioning that he would have started thinking about what was in her living will. But he didn't. Instead, I learned I could not depend on loved ones to follow through on my wishes, and I could not expect any healthcare professional to read my mind. It is my job to think ahead and figure out how to prevent many of the things that have become standard care (for example breathing and feeding tubes) at end-of-life from being done to me. Wishing myself dead or taking my own life would be antithetical to my faith and deeply held beliefs that call me to live fully all the way to the end.

My healthcare directive is the result of twenty-five years of thinking about how I would like to see the last few years of my life play out. Fortunately for me, I have found many thought leaders who affirm my rejection of a naive, persistent pursuit of longevity as a reasonable way for me to pursue my own happiness. Just because others allow medicine to do anything to them doesn't mean I must. One such thought leader is Robert M. Veatch, a pharmacist-turned-PhD in Ethics. In his book, *Patient, Heal Thyself: How the New Medicine Puts the Patient in Charge,* Veatch explains why I felt overwhelmed with grief to see my mom dying on Thanksgiving Day in 1990 and why I, a strong, healthy, accomplished forty-year old was diminished to a feeling of helplessness. He writes that while physicians focus on our medical well-being, we have to be in charge of our overall well-being.

I hope and pray that this book will help you do just that.

Hattie Bryant

CONTENTS

MOM'S STORY

ANNABELLE BRYANT, 1915-1990

It was October 9, 1990 when Dad called me to say that Mom had suffered a stroke and was in the hospital. I lived in another city and was traveling for work as a professional speaker. I made plans to get there as soon as possible. My sister lived in the same town as my parents, so the other contact made that day was to my brother, living in Hawaii at the time.

During Mom's six-week stay in the hospital and despite a busy travel schedule, I made it a point to fly in about once a week. I stayed as many days as I could before I had to fly out to my next job. I learned that when a person has a stroke, everyone watches to see what aspects of the damaged functionality will return.

In the fourth week, things got worse and she closed her eyes and didn't open them for days. The end of the fifth week of her hospitalization was Thanksgiving Day, November 22, and when I arrived, I noticed immediately that Mom's condition was very different. The first shock was her blank face. The second shock was the feeding tube; the doctors and nurses said she could no longer swallow.

My eyes told me that watching and waiting would lead to no improvement, only deterioration. I understood that doctors do what they think best, and they thought Mom needed a feeding tube. I also knew she had a living will that indicated she did not want life-prolonging care if she became incapacitated—so why was this happening? I came to learn the hard way that living wills cannot be honored unless the doctors have a copy on file.

Alone with my mom that Thanksgiving morning, I picked up the chart and found that she was being given something daily called desmopressin nasal (DDAVP nasal spray), a man-made form of a hormone that produces naturally in the pituitary gland. This hormone is important for many functions including regulating how the body uses water.

It was comforting that Mom's primary care doctor was making rounds on Thanksgiving Day. I asked him whether Mom was going to get better. The doctor said, no, this was as good as Mom was going to get. She would have to be moved to a nursing home as there was nothing more to be done for her at the hospital. Her condition was no longer acute but chronic, which meant that she could only live for a very long time with artificial feeding and the nasal spray.

I asked the doctor about the nasal spray. He said that the endocrinologist (a specialist in the area of human metabolism, especially hormones) prescribed it. The stroke had severely damaged the part of her brain that created the hormone that tells the kidneys how to handle water, and so the nasal spray was telling her kidneys to keep a proper fluid balance.

In a medical world defined more and more by specialty, treatment is often parsed out among several doctors with various areas of expertise and often without communication with other treating physicians or family before administering care. The endocrinologist probably thought he was doing the right thing and prescribing something beneficial for my mom. Or maybe he was simply doing what his training and conscience told him to do, without knowing her or her history or what her wishes or the wishes of our family, might be in this kind of situation.

I told Mom's primary doctor that I knew she didn't want to be kept alive this way and asked him to stop the nasal spray immediately. He said, "Please can you give me one more day? It is Thanksgiving and I need the hospital legal department to provide a document for your father, you, your sister and your brother to sign that will release the doctors and the hospital from any liability for the consequences due to the decision that you are making."

When I told my father about the situation later that evening, he said he agreed with me and that we needed to let her go to her forever home. Yes, she had a living will, but no one had asked for it, and he thought the doctors believed Mom was going to get better because they kept treating her.

The documents were signed the day after Thanksgiving. The nurse told us that without the nasal spray she thought it would take about one week for Mom to fully wind down out of this physical world. That is exactly what happened.

One of the benefits of the modern medical system is that there are other healthcare specialists who are involved in the patient's care *in addition to* the physician specialists. That day, the social worker for my mom's case came to the room and wanted to meet me. She took me out into the hall and said, "Everybody needs a Hattie." She is the reason for this book. Finally, I have written the book that the social worker said everybody needs.

MY PERSONAL GOALS FOR THIS BOOK

I hope that it will help you to think
about the way you want
the end of your life to play out,
that it will inspire you to tell everyone you know
what you are thinking
and, most of all,
that you will choose your own Hattie.

I hope that you will write a name on page 211,
that you will show the person you choose as your Hattie
your answers to the questions in the My Way Workbook, and
that you will then share it with your family and
healthcare providers.

It's not as hard as you might think.
You have some choices to make!

MODERN MEDICINE

When you turn the page you may be shocked. I was shocked to learn that this is the complexity I may face when I am seriously ill or have to go to a hospital due to an accident. My hope for you as you read this book is that the stories you will read and the issues raised in the next chapters will encourage you to begin the process now, whether perfectly healthy or already facing a serious, life-shortening illness. Think about, document and share the answers to the questions in the workbook at the back of the book.

MODERN MEDICAL PROBABILITIES

When you have a serious illness or suffer a trauma that lands you in the hospital, as many as a dozen physicians could be involved in your case. They each will know some aspect of your case, as they have test results that guide them to assess and address the problem they are trained to fix. They are time-pressured by today's medical environment, so they won't have much time to talk with you or even the other physicians who are on your case.

You are lost in the complexity and so is your family.

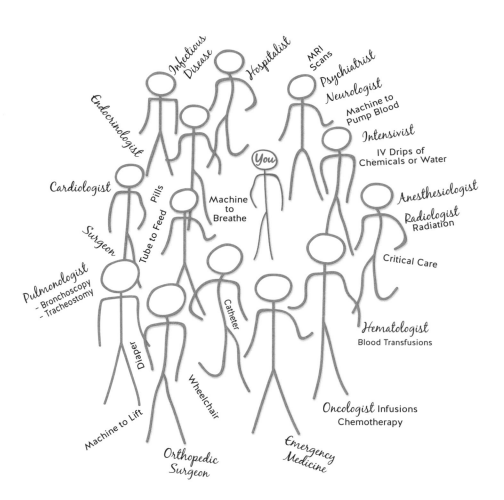

MODERN MEDICAL CAPABILITIES

You are in the hospital, you are seriously ill and you are not getting better. Do you know what's wrong? How serious it is? What your prospects for recovery are? How much have your doctors told you or your family? If there are other specialists caring for you, do they talk to you or to each other? If you are suffering despite the care you are getting, or your quality of life is poor due to a serious, perhaps life-threatening illness, you should ask for a Palliative Medicine consultation. For a complete definition please see page 149.

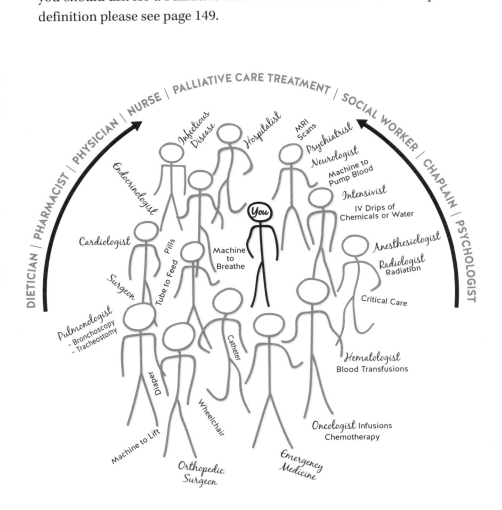

A loving couple struggled: she with many of her organs failing, he with wanting to do everything to keep her alive. She was in and out of the hospital thirty times in ten months. I was brought in to consult on the case after the twenty-eighth visit, and finally our hospitalist agreed the treatment should be stopped. This meant overriding decisions made by the nephrologist, pulmonologist, cardiologist and surgeons who were trying to please the patient's husband. She was moved to in-patient hospice care in the hospital and died two weeks later. Although her husband agreed with us that future treatments would be futile, he still feels that he killed his wife.

– PALLIATIVE CARE MANAGER

A couple heard the news that the wife had cancer. They proceeded with a few treatments then concluded that the treatments were causing more harm than good and that they would not change the outcome. They came to understand that she would never get better. They invited hospice to direct her care, which was given in her own home. When the time came close for her to die, her entire family and I were in the room. One daughter dressed her mom in her most beautiful nightgown, another daughter painted her mom's fingernails, we sang hymns and prayed until she sweetly slipped from us.

– HOSPICE NURSE

Would you want ten months of almost continuous pain, invasive treatments and living in false hope or a gentle passing?

For a full definition of the term Modern Medicine refer to the Glossary, page 147-148.

4 STEPS
TO A
PEACEFUL
DEATH

---

1 ACKNOWLEDGE THE
INEVITABILITY OF DEATH

2 UNDERSTAND THE LIMITS
OF MEDICINE

3 EDUCATE YOURSELF ABOUT
YOUR HEALTHCARE CHOICES

4 COMMUNICATE YOUR WISHES
& CHOOSE A PROXY

EVERYONE DIES

Is death optional? Of course not. Is it a choice we get to make? No. But the good news is if we think ahead, we have some choices concerning how it happens. Read on to discover the choices you can make.

From 2010-2013, Showtime aired the series *The Big C,* the story of a woman diagnosed with aggressive melanoma who seeks placement in a promising medical trial. When she finally is accepted, she learns it's only because one of the participants has died—a woman that she had overheard the doctor telling, "You are doing great." In one of the most telling scenes, she confronts this doctor, a matter-of-fact physician, and tells him that if he is going to be her doctor, he must always tell her the truth, to which he replies, "You want honesty? People die...As groundbreaking as I expect this trial to be, I'm still going to lose patients. We'll learn something from every death, so when the next patients come through, maybe they won't suffer as much, maybe they'll live longer, but make no bones about it, we all get replaced. I'm gonna die, and some other doctor will come through here and replace me...that's the truth."[1]

After fifteen years as a nurse involved in hospice and palliative care, Robin Rome says, "I have never met a person who has been ready to die. I have never met a family member who was ready for their loved one to die. I have been present at hundreds of deaths, I have consulted with dozens and dozens of physicians about end-of-life care and with families about choices and I can tell you, nearly no one is ready to die." This is what psychologists would call denial.

In his seminal work, *How We Die, Reflections on Life's Final Chapter,* Dr. Sherwin B. Nuland hits us with what his colleagues who are studying aging are discovering, "What emerges from all the experimental data and the speculations they provide is the inevitability of aging and therefore of life's finiteness."[2] And he writes, "Nature always wins in the end."[3]

Nature brings us in and nature takes us out.

BIRTH	10	20	30	40	50	60	70	80	90	DEATH
HELPLESS DEPENDENT	→ LIVE LIFE LEARNING + GROWING + HELPING OURSELVES & OTHERS →									HELPLESS DEPENDENT

"Nothing escapes the Creator's cycle. Not plants, horses, trees, birds, or human beings. Not the life of the mind. Not the life of the heart. Not the life of the spirit. All living things emerge, gather, spark new life, fall apart, die, and emerge in new ways. Each soul is a gust of God's breath unfolding in the great energy that surrounds us like an ever moving stream. The goal is not to cheat death, but to live in the stream with a humility and aliveness that only an acceptance of death can release."[4]

WHAT WE SAY WE WANT WILL PROBABLY NOT HAPPEN

If we choose to pretend that we are not going to die, then one day we could have a serious accident or get very sick and be shocked, irritated and angry about what is happening to us. This is normal. Where does normal get us? It can get us to a bad death.[5]

The data shows that most of us will be too sick to speak for ourselves at the very end. So our job[6] is to speak now, way before we get sick.[7, 8, 9] None of us know the answer to the *when, where* and *how* questions but, we all know with a 100% certainty that we are going to die.

If we live, we die; that's the rule—and there's even a mathematical formula for this developed by a gentleman named Benjamin Gompertz in 1825. "Using the Gompertz law for human mortality rates as a function of age derived from a simple model of death...in the end, no one escapes death."[10]

Nevertheless, thanks to knowledge gained largely through scientific advances, life in America today is calmer and more predictable than ever before. Maybe this lulls us into thinking that death won't come to us.[11] And while we all might be afraid of dying, or simply prefer to fantasize that seventy is the new fifty, one thing is for certain: we are not planning to die. Dr. Barron Lerner writes, "We have a culture that defies—rather than accepts—the inevitability of death. Perhaps the most famous patient in this regard was the writer Susan Sontag, who, her son later wrote, would not hear that she was dying. Sontag essentially bullied her doctors into trying all conceivable therapies for her fatal leukemia, although the treatments only prolonged her suffering."[12]

Joel Marcus, PsyD, is a psychosocial oncologist who says, "Americans feel omnipotent because we live in a rich country where all problems are solved. We have seen huge advancements in healthcare in the past fifty years so we just don't think we're going to die."[13] Dr. Marcus works with the dying every day and his entire discipline was invented because the dying were never ready to die.

BE A BOY SCOUT - BE PREPARED

You will learn in this book about the simple tools you can use to make the kind of death you want happen. These tools include a POLST and a simple directive which states your chosen proxy. That's it.

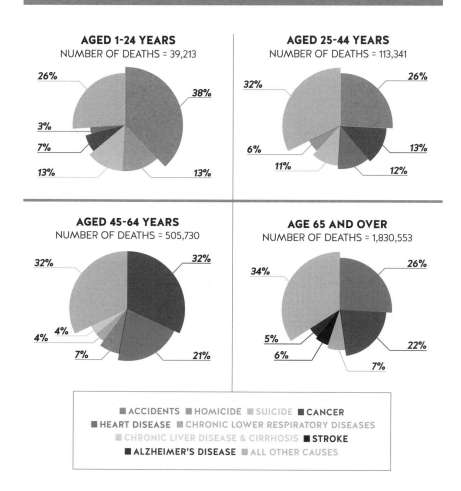

DEATH IN THE UNITED STATES[14]
Roughly speaking, the average length of life is 80 years and here we can see that our age is a factor in how we die.

AGED 1-24 YEARS
NUMBER OF DEATHS = 39,213

AGED 25-44 YEARS
NUMBER OF DEATHS = 113,341

AGED 45-64 YEARS
NUMBER OF DEATHS = 505,730

AGE 65 AND OVER
NUMBER OF DEATHS = 1,830,553

■ ACCIDENTS ■ HOMICIDE ■ SUICIDE ■ CANCER
■ HEART DISEASE ■ CHRONIC LOWER RESPIRATORY DISEASES
■ CHRONIC LIVER DISEASE & CIRRHOSIS ■ STROKE
■ ALZHEIMER'S DISEASE ■ ALL OTHER CAUSES

AGING HAPPENS

Physicist Brian Skinner, PhD writes, "By looking at theories of human mortality that are clearly wrong, we can deduce that our fast-rising mortality is not the result of a dangerous environment, but of a body that has a built-in expiration date."[15]

Anthropologists, Kristen Hawkes, Ken R. Smith and James K. Blevins write, "Increasing age brings senescence, inevitable deterioration in physiological state and functional performance. A measure of this deterioration is the rising risk of death,"[16] a journey that begins the moment we are born. Dr. Carolyn McClanahan says, "We're born terminal."[17] It's just that dying is more probable as we age, removing the common cause of death in the young like drunk driving, drug overdose, rock climbing, snowboarding, extreme mountain biking and deep ocean diving.

Professor Aaron Hagedorn says, "We cannot slow aging but we can accelerate it. We accelerate it with stress, smoking, drinking too much alcohol, taking too many drugs, not getting enough sleep and eating too much. We do not know the secret to staying young or how to avoid old age. Take away heart disease, cancer, and Alzheimer's and people still only live to 95-100 years."[18] As we age, our teeth are thinning, our gums are receding, our senses of taste and smell are diminishing, our stomach is getting thinner and on and on. Dying is a parallel process to living. When I was forty years old, I complained to my doctor that my feet hurt when I wear high heels for hours, but in high school I wore them for as many as twelve hours a day and had no pain at all. He asked me, "Do you have any gray hair?" I said, "Sure but you can't see it since it is dyed as soon as it appears." "Well," he said, "Your feet are aging, and that's why they hurt."

ACCIDENTS HAPPEN

As the chart demonstrates, the general predictors of death are age-related. For Millennials, born between the early 1980s and the early 2000s, death is not given much thought. For example, young people are more likely to die as a result of an accident or other risky behavior.

Three famous cases show that when death (or near-death) happens to the young, the line between "life" after an accident and death can be very fine indeed. Karen Ann Quinlan was only twenty-two years old in 1975 when she lost and never regained consciousness. Nancy Cruzan was twenty-six in 1983 and Terri Schiavo was twenty-seven in 1990 when they fell into vegetative states. Each of these right-to-die cases involved competing decisions about their care that led to a firestorm of controversy and tested the boundaries of legal, medical and personal ethics. Sadly, the time for them to weigh in about their personal wishes was long gone and the important decisions about their life and death were relegated to hospital administrators, lawyers and judges—making the final days and years for these young women a living hell for those who loved them most.

Tim Bowers was only thirty-two years old when he fell sixteen feet out of a tree. The injury was so severe he would live his life as a quadriplegic while his brain remained intact. His family recalled discussions he had had with his wife about not wanting to live in a wheelchair. His sister, an intensive care unit (ICU) nurse, asked him if he wanted to stay on the breathing tube and he shook his head no. Doctors asked him and they saw him shake his head no. They removed the breathing machine and seventy-five friends and family members came to the hospital to sing and pray with him during his last five hours of life.[19] Imagine yourself in Tim's situation. You probably don't have an ICU nurse sister who could understand the trajectory and complications of injuries, who could hear you say you do not want to live in a wheelchair, or who has the courage to ask the hard question and then ensure your wishes are honored to the death.

DISEASE WILL TAKE MOST OF US

A total of 2,596,993 Americans died in 2014, making the death rate 821.5 per 100,000. The average life expectancy is 78.8 years and the top five causes of death were and will continue to be in the near term: heart disease, cancer, chronic lower respiratory diseases, accidents, and strokes.[20]

Setting aside accidents and trauma, in fact 75% of all deaths of older Americans come from heart disease, cancer and stroke. Even in very old age, some specific condition will take us, because in the US we can't die of old age. A doctor is not allowed to write on our death certificate: "his heart wore out," or "she just got tired," or "he made up his mind to quit." Instead, a specific diagnosis must be stated as the cause.

We know that disease will take most of us, but we might not know that only two out of twenty of us will die quickly of our disease. A typical general physician (GP) or primary care physician has about 2,000 patients, and twenty will die each year. Just two will experience an acute event that results in death.

The other eighteen can live for years with their disease and we even know the behavior or trajectory of the diseases that kill us.

HOW PEOPLE DIE[21]

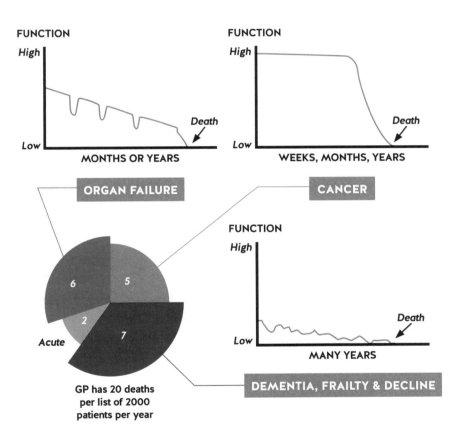

FUNCTION

High

Low

MONTHS OR YEARS

Death

ORGAN FAILURE

FUNCTION

High

Low

WEEKS, MONTHS, YEARS

Death

CANCER

FUNCTION

High

Low

MANY YEARS

Death

DEMENTIA, FRAILTY & DECLINE

Acute

6

5

2

7

GP has 20 deaths
per list of 2000
patients per year

My friend Cindy writes...
From the moment my mother died a very horrible cancer death, Dad had a request for my five siblings and me. He wanted us each to have a small stock pile of sleeping pills so that in the event he became ill and not able to take care of himself, we were to send him the pills so he could end his life. (And of course none of us could be blamed.) Now in our way of dark humor, we all joked about this for twenty years, but really it wasn't a joke. He was dead serious. Never ever did he want to be in any way incapacitated or a burden to any of us. He wanted to live his life to the fullest, and when it came to the point where his quality of life was not up to his standards, he wanted to go.

We were lucky and so was he. He had just finished a game of gin rummy with a friend, poured himself a drink of vodka with a splash of water, sat down to watch the news and died instantly of a massive heart attack. There couldn't have been a better way for him to die. He was happy, relatively healthy at the age of eighty-two, sharp, fun and funny and very much loved. I want to go the same way or at least as quickly.

(You should know that Cindy's dad took Lipitor, had a pacemaker, had bypass surgery in 1995 and a stent in 1998 then died in 2003.)

ILLNESS TRAJECTORIES[22]

It is important to study the charts on page 30. Here you can see that modern medicine is often able to pull us up and save us from death but each time we require acute care—a trip to the hospital—we never return to where we were before the event.

Cancer is complex, and it is unknown if cancers are curable at the time of first discovery. Treatments may or may not be recommended based on when in time a patient presents on the following chart. Dr. Ralph Corsetti, a surgical oncologist, says, "If one is diagnosed while on the 'flat' portion of the curve, it is not known if the cancer is curable at that point in time. This chart demonstrates the point physicians tell us that treatment will not benefit us. Notice the downward arrow. The good news is that treatments keep us optimistic and may sometimes work and be curative. At the same time, treatments can involve surgery on a vital organ or cause toxicity to the body that ultimately will not prove to be beneficial."[23]

INCURABLE CANCER TRAJECTORY DIAGNOSIS TO DEATH

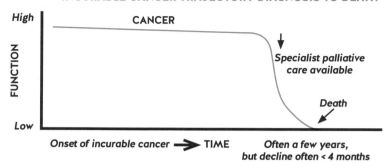

Generally predictable course, short decline
Relatively well resourced hospice care fits well

ORGAN SYSTEM FAILURE TRAJECTORY

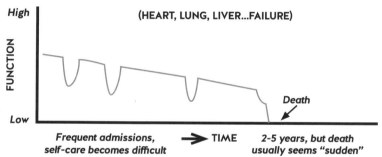

Needs: acute care for exacerbations, chronic care, support at home*
No service designed to routinely meet the needs of this pattern of decline

DEMENTIA/FRAILTY TRAJECTORY

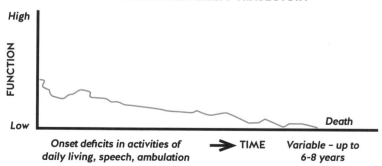

Needs: Integrated clinical care
Long term support at home, carer support, possibly nursing care
Care homes with reliably good end-of-life care

DEATH AND DYING AS A FIELD OF STUDY

Dr. Gretchen Ulfers is young, only forty years old as I write this. She is an internal medicine physician, a hospitalist and board certified in palliative and hospice medicine. In addition, she is board certified as a hospice medical director. She told me, "Dying presents a unique medical condition. The dying process is physical, psychological, social and spiritual."[24] She told me she became drawn to the dying process while working in ICU when she saw so much dying happening without proper attention being given to the non-physical aspects of death.

Dr. Michael Mitchell, like Dr. Ulfers, works only with the dying. He was drawn to his specialty because, "What we do in ICU is so often torture for patients and families. And today, there is too much being done and then too much dying in ICU."[25]

In her first book, *On Death and Dying* (published in 1969), physician Elisabeth Kübler-Ross identified five stages in the dying process: denial, anger, bargaining, depression and acceptance. One biographer writes, "She also suggested that death be considered a normal stage of life, and offered strategies for treating patients and their families as they negotiate these stages. The topic of death had been avoided by many physicians and the book quickly became a standard text for professionals who work with terminally ill patients."[26] Some say that Dr. Kubler-Ross changed the face of medicine, that she was a pioneer, and that her work was, "groundbreaking and that her book is one of the most important psychological studies of the late twentieth century."[27]

It stands to reason that, if medicine considers death to be a particular field of study, we might want to pay attention and accept that it will certainly happen to us and our loved ones and be grateful that someone is trained to help us when that time comes.

HOW WE DENY DEATH IN LIFE

Satirist P. J. O'Rourke says Baby Boomers are "a generation that is expert at lying to ourselves,"[28] which helps explain the fact that most Baby Boomers:

1. Have not saved enough to quit working—which is not so bad since we all need to keep working at something;
2. Do not have a living will, a.k.a., a healthcare directive or a healthcare proxy;
3. Have never heard of palliative care;
4. Have never heard of a POLST (Physician Orders for Life-Sustaining Treatment);
5. Have not selected a company to handle their dead body;
6. Have not decided how they want their body handled when death does come;
7. Do not have a funeral/memorial/closing party plan; and
8. Have prepared a will (60%), yet 40% have not taken this critical step in life planning.

If behavior is a clue to our priorities, then it is clear that we want the topic of death to stay off our radar screen. My mentor, Jack McNulty, internist and palliative care physician, told me he thinks people are afraid that if they talk about death they might die. Some cultures are very explicit about this belief. If we ignore "it" then it won't happen to us—especially if we're not really getting old! Tinker Bell and Peter Pan taught us in childhood that it's reasonable to act in some ways as if "I won't grow up" while conveniently ignoring the fact that life (and dying) are in fact happening while we're out making other plans.

Time won't run out for us because in the back of our minds we are hoping to outsource our death—just like we outsourced cooking to restaurants, cleaning to a paid housekeeper, the yard to the lawn care service, child-rearing to the schools and so on. Worn out parts are not causes for worry. If someone else dies, we get their heart, kidney or whatever piece we need! That's how we think it might work. There is always a new drug and more sophisticated technology to try.[29]

DEATH DENIAL IS NEW AND CONVENIENT

Denying death makes us different from our ancestors. Philippe Aries writes, "For thousands of years man was lord and master of his death, and the circumstances surrounding it. Today this has ceased to be so. It used to be understood and accepted that man knew when he was dying whether he became spontaneously aware of the fact or whether he had to be told."[31]

By the twentieth century, Sigmund Freud proposed that we tend to protect ourselves with a set of defense mechanisms. While denial can be a healthy short-term response to bad news, it becomes unhealthy if we hold on to it so long that truth is never allowed to surface. Aries says, "Whereas denial may serve a useful protective purpose early on, it may become maladaptive if maintained over prolonged periods of time."[32]

A woman I will call Marianne was called to her mother's deathbed and told by healthcare providers that her mother only had a few hours to live. Marianne wanted to tell her mother goodbye, to say thank you for what her mother had done for her and to somehow achieve closure with her. Instead, when Marianne started speaking, her mother said, in typical denial fashion, "Get me my mascara. I need my mascara." While applying the mascara, her mother died.

It's no wonder we are such "deniers," when our brains are wired for survival! As infants we instinctively adapt coping mechanisms such as pleasing, acting needy, manipulating and controlling, withdrawing, or bullying to keep the adults in our lives caring for and loving us so we can grow into adulthood. Our instinct is also to avoid pain, so we become masters of denial. Death certainly appears to be the opposite of survival, and it is an unknown experience we fear. We must mature and grasp that letting go of denial is the path to being fully alive in the present moment—this truth will allow us to make choices and gain some measure of control in approaching death, that mysterious threshold we all ultimately face.

– Dr. Linda M. Fischer, PhD, LMFT[33]

While Freud concerned himself with how individuals use denial as a defense mechanism, sociologists have been busy studying our death-denying society. Camilla Zimmermann and Gary Rodin write, "This characterization, which sociologists have termed the 'denial of death thesis,' first arose in the social science, psychological and clinical medical literature between 1955 and 1985."[34] Philippe Aries explains, "(The) sociology of death was begun in 1955 with Geoffrey Gorer's comprehensive article, 'The Pornography of Death'."[35] Mr. Gorer explains, "During the last half-century, public health measures and improved preventive medicine have made natural death among the younger members of the population much more uncommon than it had in earlier periods, so that a death in the family—save in the fullness of time—became a relatively uncommon incident in home life...(at the same time) violent death has played an ever-growing part in the fantasies offered to mass audiences—detective stories, thrillers, Westerns, war stories, spy stories, science fiction, and eventually horror comics."[36]

Adults alive today would have to agree that we have seen more death on screens than we have in our home. As media images of death have increased, death has become a professionally managed event in the hospital and far removed from the public's sight. The depictions of graphic, violent death in the media—Gorer labeled the images pornographic—are false. He is saying that the death our culture "knows" about is what Hollywood tells us it is.

After Gorer came Herman Feifel's work.[37] A researcher, he wondered why the death of 50,000,000[38] people in World War II had not prompted scholars to learn what people thought about death and dying. He organized a symposium on the psychology of death and dying which took place at the American Psychological Association convention in 1956 and included experts in anthropology, psychiatry, art, literature, religion, philosophy, psychobiology and theology.

His book, *The Meaning of Death,* published in 1959, is a compilation of writings by thought leaders from a range of disciplines. It is still considered a "central resource to the field it helped to generate."[39] Feifel's own research revealed some interesting if not surprising conclusions such as the fact that religious persons are more afraid of death than non-religious persons.[40] In 1965 Feifel noted, "death anxiety in physicians was higher than in non-physician caregivers. He speculated that some physicians sought medical careers to help curb their own unrecognized death anxiety."[41]

LIVING IN THE TENSION

The tension is this—we are living and dying right now. Rick Warren writes, "Longing for the ideal while criticizing the real is evidence of immaturity. On the other hand, settling for the real without striving for the ideal is complacency. Maturity is living with the tension."[42]

Someday we will be told that our life is ending. Listen hard, then step away and ask yourself: Do I want to have the most days possible or to die gently? Do I want to go softly with care, or do I want to spend weeks, months or maybe years living a medicalized life,[43] which may be a prolonged dying process? Do I want my only appointments to be with doctors and lab technicians or do I want to spend that time with family and friends sharing and making memories? Letting go of desperate measures can give us more time to say, "Thank you" and "I love you" and untether us to do other things more meaningful to ourselves and those in our circles of family, friendship and care.

STEP 1 in taking control of end-of-life decisions is acceptance of the plain truth that death will happen to us and to all of our loved ones. To take this step toward greater peace of mind, please answer the questions and fill in the blanks you will find on pages 184-191 of the MY WAY WORKBOOK.

4 STEPS
TO A
PEACEFUL
DEATH

---

1 ACKNOWLEDGE THE
INEVITABILITY OF DEATH

2 UNDERSTAND THE LIMITS
OF MEDICINE

3 EDUCATE YOURSELF ABOUT
YOUR HEALTHCARE CHOICES

4 COMMUNICATE YOUR WISHES
& CHOOSE A PROXY

CHAPTER 2

MEDICINE HAS ITS LIMITS

Having attributed a growing discomfort the day before to "indigestion" following a hamburger with onions for lunch, at 2:45 AM on September 24, 1955, President Dwight Eisenhower complained that he had a pain in his chest. After listening to the President's heart at 3:11 AM, Dr. Howard McCrum Snyder, the president's personal physician, determined that Eisenhower had experienced an injury to his heart. Eisenhower later recalled, "Subconsciously, every healthy man thinks of serious illness as something that happens occasionally—but always to other people. But when, after spending a most uncomfortable night under sedation, I awakened to the realization that I was in an oxygen tent with doctors and nurses in attendance, I had thrust upon me the unpleasant fact that I was, indeed, a sick man."[44]

At the strong advice of his doctors, President Eisenhower had already given up his four packs of cigarettes per day.[45] Now, upon the counsel of the special physiologist Dr. Ancel Keys who had been brought in to consult on the president's condition, Eisenhower had to give up bacon and eggs. The media published Dr. Keys' findings on the front page—Animal fat kills us—and the president of the United States was now stuck with a diet of grapefruit and dry Melba Toast™.[46] President Eisenhower's health situation "was given a prominent place in the news; it was detailed and reiterated through all major mass media."[47] If the American general who led the forces that turned the tide to defeat Hitler was eating dry melba toast, maybe that's what we all needed to eat.

While the health of our leaders has always been of great public interest, the marriage of modern medicine and instant access to information has created a pair of rose-colored glasses for those of us alive in the twenty-first century. No need to hope for a miracle cure anymore; medicine delivers one over and over and over again. Pains are relieved, joints re-built, blood vessels and valves replaced, every breath enhanced and every infection knocked out.[48, 49, 50] So optimistic are we that our greatest illness may be our delusion about just how powerful modern medicine truly is.

> An astonishing 40% of Americans believe that medical technology can always save their lives. The old joke that Americans believe death is just one more disease to be cured is no longer a joke. No wonder Brookings Institution economist Henry Aaron—who has prominently called attention to all the problems of technology—has nonetheless written that any effort to curb the introduction of new technologies "beyond what is required for safety and efficacy would be sheer madness."[51]

Doctors see us and doctors fix us.[52] They make it look easy because their knowledge and training prepares them for what we present to them. Dr. Elizabeth Chaitin told me, "People actually think that if they find the right hospital and the right doctor that they do not have to be sick or die."[53]

"Hospitals have been called the modern equivalent of Renaissance cathedrals, which were important commercial centers as well as a place of solace and hope in the face of death. That would make Johns

Hopkins the Vatican of hospitals, the site of some of the most significant milestones in modern medicine, including the development of the radical mastectomy, open-heart surgery on blue babies, and kidney dialysis."[54] Dr. Richard Della Penna told me that physicians tease about the letters MD. With a laugh in his voice he said, "Didn't you know that MD means MedicalDiety?"[55] Yet, while we consider doctors the high priests of our one true, evidence-based religion, doctors do sometimes have to admit that medicine, scientific research and life is still filled with mystery that even all the knowledge and technology of modern medicine cannot explain.[56, 57, 58, 59, 60]

SPARED BY MODERN MEDICINE

Most of us had childhoods that were very different from our parents'. Consider these remarkable medical advances that have saved the greatest generation and now us, just within the past seventy years:

- Just three years before the first Baby Boomer was born, penicillin arrived in time to save the lives of thousands of Allied soldiers—starting with those injured on D-Day, 1944.
- Another big life-saver came with the invention of the influenza vaccine in 1945. It's hard for us to imagine this, but half of our soldiers who died in World War I were taken out by the flu, not a bullet.[61]
- In 1955, American children started receiving Jonas Salk's polio vaccine.[62] Thanks to Dr. Salk, very few of us experienced the painful, metal braces that supported President Franklin D. Roosevelt and so many others afflicted by this crippling disease.
- In 1963, a live measles vaccine was introduced, reversing the nearly unfathomable fact that in the 1950s and 1960s, measles killed nearly twice as many children as polio.[63]
- As late as 1971, the measles vaccine was combined with the MMR vaccine to include mumps and rubella (also called German measles), three mostly ignored, but previously deadly childhood diseases.

From such early medical miracles grew our love affair with the entire healthcare system and with our pharmacists and physicians in particular. Our confidence in medicine flows from our collective migration away from anything that requires trust or faith toward everything that supplies hard-core data—and doctors have the data. What we have lost during this migration is our common sense. Instead, we indulge in any solution/option/care that is presented with data,[64] then rush to grab and pay up for every health-related miracle cure or drug that comes down the new product development pipeline.[65] Too bad the data is cherry-picked for marketing soundbites and spin, so what we think is evidence-based information may not represent what the touted study's authors actually intended to convey as actionable.

We are oversold,[66] over-diagnosed,[67, 68] over-treated[69] and most of all, over-confident that modern medicine has a cure for whatever ails you. Slick television ads convince us we might be sick or abnormal. Seeing our partner's suggestive glance didn't elicit the expected physical response. Or that nagging feeling; it is perfectly described by the cartoon woman with the elephant's foot on her chest.[70, 71] So, we become worried and believe that no matter the malady—real or imagined—there's a cure for it. Is this helpful to our well-being or just the result of marketing genius run amok between our healthcare system and the patient who is now being treated as the consumer? Primary care physicians know that the "worried well" consume thirty to 60% of their time.[72] The physician has to listen to the patient who is drowning in data—from television and the Internet—but has no actionable information. Just to pacify the "worried well," the physician might write a prescription that he or she knows will do no good but probably no harm either.

THE HEART OF THE MATTER

About 2.5 million Americans die each year; and in spite of all our medical knowledge and miracles, almost 25% (600,000) of these deaths are from heart disease. Perhaps this statistic is not so surprising considering we have 60,000 miles of blood vessels[73] and 100 trillion cells,[74] all nourished by an organ that will beat about 2.5 billion times if we live to be eighty years old. It is the vital pump that moves life-sustaining oxygen through those 60,000 miles, without which we die. That's a lot of action, and in the US alone 300,000 hearts stop dead each year.[75]

It's no surprise that this vital organ has been the source of so much research. The first implantable pacemaker[76] was introduced in 1958. In 1967, the world was stunned to learn of the first human heart transplant. As much as by the miracle of the surgery itself, the public was smitten by the handsome South African surgeon, Dr. Christiaan Barnard, whose made-for-TV good looks and voice seemed all part of the greater-than-life package designed for such miracles. He wrote, "On December 3, 1967, the heart of a girl who died from a brain injury was transplanted to a patient suffering from heart disease that, until then, had proved untreatable."[77]

This was a man who looked and sounded like God. With his long white starched coat and reserved, but very official manner, he shaped an entire generation's view of "The Doctor." He was the man who could take a healthy heart from a dead person and replace the dying heart of a living person to sustain that life. As unbelievable as the act, the promise it held for the future of medicine and the health of future generations was the real miracle.

Just two years later, the public would witness another miracle with the introduction of cardio pulmonary resuscitation (CPR), a 15 to 30 minute procedure in which the chest is pressed on forcefully (enough to crush the sternum and ribs of an elderly patient), and may include electric stimulation to the chest and special medicines, as well as a tube inserted through the mouth or nose into the lung and connected to a breathing machine.[78]

This procedure was initially for witnessed cardiac arrest but today CPR is always applied unless there is an order *not* to do it. As a consequence, people with advanced years and those with advanced chronic conditions receive it, even though there is no chance it will have a positive effect on those who are dying or even dead.

Dr. John P. "Jack" McNulty, a physician since 1951, believes that a new level of regard and fascination with science and a physician's ability ticked up to *beyond-mortal* due to the introduction of CPR. He has practiced internal medicine and palliative care for sixty years and today he teaches other physicians and palliative care teams. His assessment of this event deserves consideration.

> The first successful use of cardiopulmonary resuscitation (CPR) was a watershed moment in medicine. This changed everything. I was there. I watched as the public was swept up. The public's reaction to CPR was misunderstood. In 1969 the media spread the word that a man who was dead was 'brought back to life.' This made the news and the public went crazy and started demanding CPR. There was a euphoria that overtook the country. People started believing that death is optional.[79]

Based upon the miraculous success of the first CPR procedure on a strong and generally healthy man in his 50s, soon every healthcare professional in every hospital was required to perform CPR on every patient who stopped breathing or whose heart stopped beating, even though,

> pressing on the chest can cause a sore chest, broken ribs or a collapsed lung. Patients with breathing tubes usually require medicine to keep them comfortable. Most patients who survive will need to be on a breathing machine in the intensive care unit to help their breathing for a while.

> Few patients (less than 10%) in the hospital who have CPR survive and are able to function the way they used to. Many patients live for a short time after CPR, but still die in the hospital. Patients who have many illnesses usually don't survive. Almost no one with advanced cancer survives CPR and lives long enough to leave the hospital. Of the few patients who do, many continue to become weak or have brain damage. Some patients may need to live on a breathing machine for the rest of their lives. CPR may also prolong the dying process.[80]

Passion and necessity are the mothers of invention. The physician who invented CPR, anesthesiologist, Dr. Peter Safar,[81] was not trying to cut God out or pretend to be God—he was thinking constantly about how to help his daughter. Dr. Safar had one child that suffered from asthma. He and his wife had to help their daughter breathe through every night of her short life. She died at the age of eleven from an asthma attack while her parents were attending a conference.[82]

Not everyone was a devotee of the new fail-safe, life-saving procedure. Dr. Pat Gary, a third-generation physician, relates that her father, who spent much of his time in a hospital taking care of his patients, would turn and walk away when he heard Code Blue (the hospital emergency code indicating a patient needing immediate resuscitation). Though he never said it out loud, Dr. Gary got the impression that her father thought there was something terribly wrong with CPR. Similarly, in an essay that draws on his book, *The Good Doctor: A Father, A Son and the Evolution of Medical Ethics*, Dr. Barron Lerner tells of how in 1996 his physician father "...had single-handedly prevented other physicians from performing CPR on a woman whose heart had just stopped. He actually laid his body on top of hers to ensure they couldn't try."[83]

Were Drs. Gary and Lerner's fathers stuck in the past and not open to the newest techniques and treatments? Not at all. Their physician children now look back on their fathers with great respect and even envy the kind of clear thinking that kept the old doctors grounded in what is best for their patients. New medicine is about speed, efficiency and fixing a specific problem while the old way was more about the patient as person—a whole person. As Dr. Barron Lerner recounts his own medical practice and reasoning with regard to CPR, "I did see patients where I felt that resuscitation was inappropriate. They were so end-stage and in such suffering that it just seemed, as my dad would've said, 'It is inhumane to pound on their chest and break their ribs.'"[84]

CPR saves lives and is valuable when the patient is strong and healthy enough to live through to the other side of the ordeal. If any of us call 911, the emergency personnel who respond to the call are obligated to administer CPR if breathing has stopped and this is good in most situations. If a person stops breathing in a hospital or any professionally managed care facility, CPR is applied with no questions asked. However, there will come a time when you might not want this done to you. You can use the workbook to help you sort this out for yourself.

In 1974, when my Uncle Dru was fifty-four years old, he had some chest pains. He was admitted to the hospital for tests and while on the treadmill he had a massive heart attack. It was code blue. With CPR they got his heart beating but oxygen had been lost to the brain and he lived for seven years in a vegetative state. My aunt said that once in awhile he would babble and she thinks that one time she heard him say, "Die me."

The last time I saw him he was skin and bones and tied down to the bed. He had a feeding tube he did not like and he kept pulling it out, they said. When his kidney started to fail my aunt finally said, "Please remove the feeding tube." Until that moment my aunt didn't have the confidence to speak up and during the entire process. No one gave her a choice.

Sadly, hospice didn't receive its rightful respect or funding until 1982, which means my adorable Uncle Dru had his heart attack eight years too soon. Or, if he had had it before 1969 he would not have been "brought back to life" and would never have been tied down to a bed.

THE FAT OF THE MATTER

In 1957 Dr. Keys, the same physician who told the president to stop eating butter, wrote an article "Diet and the Epidemiology of Coronary Heart Disease," published by the *Journal of American Medical Association,* that concluded "cholesterol levels cannot be satisfactorily controlled unless the saturated fat intake is reduced."[85]

Dr. Dudley White was also one of the founders of the American Heart Association and was convinced by Dr. Keys' research. Because there was great public pressure to come out with strong recommendations about diet, he was able, over considerable objection, to get his "theory" accepted at the 1984 "consensus committee" hearings on diet. The "diet-heart hypothesis" was born.[86]

Building on some of this earlier research, President Nixon (Eisenhower's vice president) decided the US needed national guidelines[87] for nutrition. He put then Senator George McGovern in charge of the newly formed US Senate Select Committee on Nutrition and Human Needs. In 1977, the committee said to avoid becoming overweight, "Americans should consume only as much energy as they expended."[88]

What is our condition since President Eisenhower put heart disease on the front page and the government told us how to eat? Fatter than ever. As John Tierney puts it in his article, "Diet and Fat: a Severe Case of Mistaken Consensus," "The notion that fatty foods shorten your life began as a hypothesis based on dubious assumptions and data; when scientists tried to confirm it, they failed repeatedly."[89, 90, 91, 92]

A RULE FOR IMMORTALITY IS DEBUNKED

The 2015 US Dietary Guidelines rescind the warnings that eating cholesterol rich food will kill you.[93] However, those of us who have been paying attention to dietary research started noticing a shift in thinking on this topic years ago. The November 14, 2013 headline of an article published by MedScape.com read "New Cholesterol Guidelines Abandon LDL Targets." Paul J. Rosch, MD and president of the American Institute of Stress wrote an article, "Why Stress is a Far More Important Cause of Coronary Disease than Cholesterol." He asserted, "High cholesterol does not increase risk for heart attacks in people older than sixty-five, healthy women of any age, nor in patients with diabetes or renal failure. Senior citizens with higher cholesterol have significantly fewer infections and live longer than those with lower cholesterol."[94]

The anonymous nurse who became famous on the Internet by writing about her own heart attack said, "Research has discovered that a cholesterol elevated reading is rarely the cause of a myocardial infarction (MI or heart attack) unless it's unbelievably high and/or accompanied by high blood pressure. MIs are usually caused by long-term stress and inflammation in the body, which dumps all sorts of deadly hormones into your system to sludge things up in there."[95] Her point is that just because you have low cholesterol doesn't mean you will not have a heart attack.

If by chance we have some arteries that clog and impede the blood supply, the work of the heart's pumping muscle, doctors can re-inflate them thanks to the invention of the first balloon angioplasty by German doctors in 1977. The success of this treatment led to the coronary stent. These procedures have formed a new category called interventional cardiology. "By 1997, angioplasty had become one of the most common medical interventions in the world."[96]

If the heart merely beats irregularly, you can have a pacemaker installed that will keep you from losing a beat.[97] While the pacemaker is for a slow heart affecting the upper chambers of your heart, the implantable cardioverter-defibrillator is for the heart that is beating too fast or the heart that just likes to stop completely.[98] The LVAD (left ventricular assist device) is a recent heart saver implanted in tandem with the heart to support circulation. Physicians predict its use to increase as a bridge or even an alternative to heart transplantation.[99]

If a physician tells me that I need one of these devices, I will stop and think hard and I think you should, too. My study for this book has not made me dislike physicians—quite the opposite. I have grown to love so many of them. However, no physician is going to live my life for me and it is smart for us all to think for ourselves and make decisions based upon our personal dreams and goals. I promise that your physician wants the best for you, but treatments, pills, devices and procedures are harder to take than to give. My friend and orthopedic surgeon, John Cazale, has performed hundreds of knee and hip replacement surgeries but things changed for him last year when he had his own knees replaced. He said, "Now I truly know how my patients feel. This is harder than I had imagined!" Nurses tell me that patients and families so often do not understand the implications of treatments and that what might seem like the perfect solution creates new sets of problems.

A palliative care nurse told me this story about a recent case she handled in a large urban hospital. A seventy-four-year-old man said yes to an LVAD and his wife was his designated caregiver. Over the next twenty-three months he was admitted to the hospital fifteen times, all due to his heart failure. His wife died sixteen months after the LVAD implantation and his drive line became chronically infected. The drive line is a tube that passes from the device through the skin and is connected to an external controller and power source. On his last admission to the hospital, the man asked that the LVAD be turned off because he was constantly weak; he was breathless and fatigued; he could not take a shower or go fishing. With his wife gone, his daughter was his caregiver. He didn't want her to have the burden any longer, and he was tired of it all. The physician said, "I'm shocked. You've done so well for nearly two years!" The physician refused the man's request. The man was discharged to his home with hospice who assisted with discontinuing the LVAD.

A girlfriend watched as her mom's life was diminished by dementia. In a care facility that she would visit almost daily, her mom was just barely breathing. The mom had a pacemaker that required replacement after so many years. The procedure to replace the pacemaker was done even though I'm not sure who said that was OK to do to a woman who had lost her cognitive functioning. When my girlfriend's sister came from out of town to visit, the sister quietly put a pillow over her mother's head. Wouldn't allowing the pacemaker to run down so the mom could die naturally have been a better approach?

To have as much control as possible over our own death, we have to consider carefully the consequences of saying yes. For me, how I live my life is much more important to me than how long I live.

A DRUG FOR WHAT AILS YOU

The 1960s drug culture, whether we were active participants or not, was instrumental in the utilization, legitimization and rationalization for today's commercialized drugs. What hallucinogens did for our minds in the 1960s and 1970s, statins are doing for our high cholesterol and hearts today.[100] A prescription for statins means we can take a pill and engage in the mind-bending practice of eating anything because we would rather take a pill than do what is necessary for a healthy lifestyle. My surgeon friend likes to laugh at himself. He says it's so much easier to tell patients what to do than to do what he tells the patients to do. He pleads with patients to get to and stay at a healthy weight and to do some kind of exercise. He gets his exercise on a racing bike but, in the back of his mind, he knows if he can't control his cholesterol naturally, he can take a statin. It's fun for me to have so many physicians as friends and to realize that modern medicine is just as alluring to them as it is to the rest of us.

My dad was always watching his weight and I got his short, stocky build. In 1970, a college professor taught me something I'll never forget. One day, he told our class that he had gone to purchase a new suit and his usual size was too small. He said that years ago he made a rule: never go up a size, go home and lose weight. That has worked for me in addition to being a jogger/race walker since 1975. I asked my friend and neighbor who is a cardiologist to tell me all about statins and he said you do not have to be overweight to benefit. He said, "Do not make any aspect of healthcare sound like it can be reduced to black and white. When I first started practicing medicine, I was running to the ER constantly to meet patients who were having heart attacks. Now the calls are less frequent. I believe statin use has contributed to this reduction. Sure, there are side effects with statin drugs that may occur but I work to find the right statin for each patient."

SOLUTIONS COMING AT US FROM EVERY DIRECTION

The mix of drugs, treatments and interventional surgeries is working, and it is reported that "while cardiovascular mortality is down, patients in need are on the rise."[101] We, the Baby Boomers, are the patients in need. With the years piling up, the problems pile on, and our heart takes the beating. Also, the cardiovascular interventions delay the effects of the underlying condition—fewer die from myocardial infarctions and more die from chronic heart failure.

We are grateful to the heart-part healers. It is ironic though that when people are asked how they want to die, after the most common response to "die in my sleep," the next largest group say they want to live fully, then drop dead. Physicians I interviewed said, "I want to play a great game of basketball then collapse leaving the court," or, "I want to be mountain climbing and drop dead." But if I stop taking piles of pills at the age of 65 and if I refuse pacemakers, and other forms of medical intervention, I have a better chance of going out before I have to endure years of a medicalized life. It's a choice any of us are free to make, but today it seems we are considered crazy if we choose less medicine.

SUGAR AND SITTING MADE US FAT AND SICK

When I was born in 1950, the US did not have rampant public health problems of obesity and diabetes. Now we do.[102] Dr. Arthur Agatston says that sitting in front of televisions and computers along with consuming fast food and not getting enough sleep means "...our toxic lifestyle is trumping our advances in medical science."[103] In fact, the American Cancer Society reports that sitting for six or more hours daily can elevate your chances of dying from cancer and other major diseases—even if you maintain a healthy weight and don't smoke. The study found that for men, the risk of death increased by 17%, and for women, an alarming 37%. It's worse yet for those who do not regularly exercise and who sit for long periods per day face even greater mortality rates—a startling 94% for women and 49% for men. Who knew that one of the easiest and healthiest things we could do was get off our derrière?[104, 105]

As if our sedentary lifestyles aren't deadly enough, let's take a look at the crippling effects of our appetite for sugar. American ingenuity has found countless ways and forms to inject it into our diets so that we're all junkies. Who would have thought that my hamburger would be better with, indeed require, a healthy splash of ketchup (sugar is ingredient number three) to make it more pleasing?

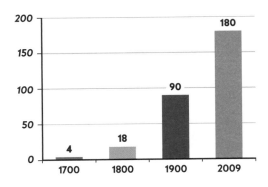

REFINED SUGAR CONSUMPTION TRENDS AVERAGE
POUNDS/PERSON/YEAR

Not only does it taste good, it sends specific instructions to our brain that we should keep eating.[106] No matter what we call it—corn syrup, fructose, dextrose—there is no sugar coating for the deadly implications of a sugar-loaded diet.

In 1890, the obesity rate in the US for white males in their fifties was 3.4%. In 1975, the obesity rate in the US was 15%. In 2014, 34.9% or 78.6 million of Americans were obese.[107] In 1893, there were fewer than three diabetics per 100,000 people in US. Today, there are 8,000 diabetics per 100,000 people in US.[108] We don't need to be skinny to die in peace, and of course we are free to eat and sit then deal with the consequences as we age. Extra weight wears out our hearts and our joints. Diabetes takes a toll on heart and blood vessels, eyes, kidneys, nerves and even our gums and teeth. I happen to know from a trusted source that the executives at one of the companies that makes diabetes medications and devices thinks it is funny that Americans are so good at making them rich. The more we eat, the richer the drug makers get.

If we choose to die naturally, being overweight is no problem. It's just that death might come a bit sooner due to the stress extra weight puts on our bodies.

CANCER SURVIVORS ARE EVERYWHERE

Cancer used to kill most people. The first death that touched my life was in 1963 when my girlfriend's mom died from cervical cancer. We were thirteen years old and the family was so distraught they forgot about my girlfriend's planned Bat Mitzvah.

Since then, as many people survive a cancer diagnosis as die from it. The survivors are proud and loud and they should be. In the seventies, one out of every two survived for five years, now more than two out of three survive that long.[109]

The strategies for getting rid of cancer still include surgery, chemotherapy and radiation, and the doctors have learned to target their treatments with ever-improving drugs and technology due to increased government attention and funding. President Nixon signed the National Cancer Act in 1971, and since then hundreds of millions of dollars have flowed to fight "The War on Cancer."[110] With money and time, researchers have developed the tools used today that can detect cancer early which is why many of us know someone who has "beat it."

FINDING MORE CANCER

Dr. H. Gilbert Welch, one of the authors of *Over-Diagnosed, Making People Sick in the Pursuit of Health* says, "I believe over-diagnosis is the biggest problem posed by modern medicine. It is a problem relevant to virtually all medical conditions. It has led millions of people to become patients unnecessarily, to be made anxious about their health, to be treated needlessly and to bear the inconvenience and financial burdens associated with over-diagnosis."[111]

He describes how a friend, a fellow physician and oncologist, got a PSA test—screening for prostate cancer— annually. One year the number was a bit too high, so this friend had biopsies taken and one out of ten showed some cancer, so he went for the radical prostatectomy. He thought it would be an easy procedure but it wasn't.[112]

When the friend asked Dr. Welch what he would have done had he received the same PSA result, Dr. Welch said he would have done nothing because he does not get screened for prostate cancer. He goes on to report that 80% of men over seventy who are screened for prostate cancer have it and only 3% will ever die of it. This is because, "some cancers don't progress at all. Some cancers will never make a difference to patients."[113]

In January 2014, *The BMJ* (originally called the *British Medical Journal*) reported that over a twenty-five-year period mammography was no better than an old fashioned check-up at finding breast cancer and preventing death.[114] At the same time, the imaging is so precise that conditions were found in breasts that scared everyone into unnecessary procedures.

Just like we can have chronic heart disease and chronic diabetes, you can live with chronic cancer. Oncologists will tell you they can "control" the cancer. Instead of dying from it you can have it cut out, poisoned out, or burned out. And then by taking drugs the rest of your life, it can be kept out or starved of blood supply to make it a manageable size. The older we get the harder this is, so if your neighbor who is forty is living with cancer, this doesn't mean that when you're sixty-five or seventy-five you will too. Age matters when our bodies break for any reason.

My great niece broke her arm when she was fifteen years old. In six weeks she was back fully engaged as a star athlete on her school volleyball team. In October of 2014, I fractured my tibia. It was fun until it happened because I was trying to keep up with one of my four nieces as we rode scooters around Bermuda. My doctor and friend, orthopedic surgeon John Cazale, said, "Your knee is healing nicely. You can see from the X-ray that the bone is closing. Look at me. Your knee will never again be the way God made it. You can never again jump up and down, jog, do squats or lunges." While I may accept these limitations to an otherwise active lifestyle, ten months later, my knee is still full of fluid and it still hurts. Dr. Cazale told me to take two Advil® twice a day until the healing is complete.

Disease is different for those of us who are Baby Boomers and older. More than one physician told me that if a person can't walk a quarter of a mile, they probably won't do well taking chemotherapy. For sure, if I am ever too frail to walk and I get incurable cancer, I think I'll take a pass on the chemo cocktail. I prefer Grey Goose®.

Dr. Charles von Gunten, oncologist and palliative medicine physician, agrees that, "The ability to walk is part of what oncologists call 'performance status'—which is a measure of your sum total of ability to live your life in a normal way. Many oncologists use the ability to walk into the office as a proxy for a more detailed assessment. But the bottom line issue is that people who are weak and frail aren't helped by standard chemotherapy—it kills them quicker. People who are 'fit' are more likely to be benefitted." [115]

Dr. Daniel Matlock told me, "If you've seen one cancer, you've seen one cancer. Some are completely curable while others can act like chronic diseases. Others, like lung and pancreas tend to be relentless—those are the ones I've really seen patients get tortured with chemotherapy. There are less toxic treatments such as hormone blockers that even the frail can benefit from. This is tough. My grandfather had metastatic prostate cancer for seventeen years that was kept completely at bay with hormones. He's lucky, but not a huge outlier. At the same time we torture people with other cancers with false hope that they will get something like my grandfather experienced. And that is what I am trying to address here. I counsel my patients to go to oncologists to get their impressions, ask questions, thank them and don't accept their word as gospel." [116]

Dr. Jack McNulty warns us all that, "Some cancers are rapidly fatal; some are cured, and some are kept in remission by longer-term treatment. With the long-term survival, it is reasonable to believe that the body's ability to avoid decline and death is diminished with increased age by failing immune function, resistance to therapy, or other complicating illnesses."

"When the time comes and you need careful evaluation for a serious illness, find a physician who cares enough about you and your problem to guide you through the process."[117] – DR. JACK MCNULTY

MADISON AVENUE IN THE EXAM ROOM

In 1995, the Federal Drug Administration modified its rules for direct-to-consumer broadcast advertising.[118] Though the ailments described in the ads have existed all of our lives—high blood pressure, depression, high cholesterol, diabetes—suddenly they seem new. So we buy the Big Pharma marketing pitch hook, line and sinker, and then expect/convince/demand our doctor to write us a prescription. As a result, Madison Avenue and its advertising wizards make it all quite American to spend $329.2 billion on medications.[119] We are consumers. It's part of what makes us Americans! More is better and the newest is better than the old. We are caught up in innovation which in so many ways is wonderful and fun.

In our free-market system, a smart person can make something and try to sell it to us. We are free to buy it or not buy it. Today, we are buying every pill, every patch, every treatment and every promise the product makers of modern medicine can dream up.[120] We need to ask if these promises are accurate or if they come at a higher personal cost to us than is indicated.

So many of us have defaulted to the lazy ways of pill popping.[121] We have not taken the road less traveled of moderation in all things, but rather, the one paved with unhealthy diets, unhealthy habits and prescriptions, choosing to ignore the warning signs along the way. Ambien, the billion-dollar sleeping pill, is now known for "triggering bizarre behavior" like eating buttered cigarettes or shooting people dead with a gun. Allison McCabe reported in 2009 that Robert Stewart killed eight people and injured two when he opened fire in a nursing home. He was trying to kill his wife but she hid in a bathroom. His defense attorney argued that he was under the influence of Ambien which resulted in the charges being changed from first-degree to second-degree murder. His sentence was 142-179 years in prison. Ms. McCabe goes on to write, "Ambien users sued Sanofi because of bizarre sleep-eating behaviors while on the drugs. According to Chana Lask, attorney for the class action suit, people were eating things like buttered cigarettes and eggs, complete with shells, while under the influence of Ambien."[122] There was always the warning on the label but people still took the pill in true invincible twenty-first century style.

Modern medicine is so addicting, we run to it, fund it,[123, 124, 125] donate to it,[126, 127, 128] and are proud when our children choose to study it. But, can too much of a good thing prop us up and keep us from a gentle death? Can we have too much ice cream, too much technology, too much sun, too much medicine? We are so fussy over ourselves and we have forgotten that we have an internal governor. We run after this and that and maybe we need to sit quietly and listen to our own pulse.

Dr. Laura Morrison told me, "The decades-long experiment we've been running to medicalize living and dying has failed us as it often keeps us from having meaning all the way to the end. Our system is set up for us to all die in ICU. I think it is due to our inability to have the hard discussion and more skillfully and intentionally integrate technology and progress into the natural rhythm of our life cycle."[129]

A SOLUTION LOOKING FOR A PROBLEM

It is difficult to know just how many more misleading studies are guiding our health purchase decisions, but based on the constant barrage of television, magazine and pop-up messages we receive, there are countless providers who are all too happy to sell us a solution. And this perspective on an opportunity waiting to happen is not new. In *Selling Sickness,* the authors recount the dream of Henry Gadsen, the pharmaceutical giant Merck's CEO from 1965-1975. Mr. Gadsen made it clear that he wanted his company's products to be as common as Wrigley's chewing gum, a rather prescient ambition considering the following. On one day in 2003, it was estimated that 8,010,000 women had osteoporosis. Literally, the next day, the number had grown to an astonishing 14,791,000.[130] This was because the National Osteoporosis Foundation decided that women with T scores (a measure of bone density) -2.0 should be treated rather than the old guideline for treatment which was set at -2.5. With enough money, time and research, American pharmaceutical ingenuity can come up with ways to make us a patient from now until the end of our life.[131]

This table shows the effect of lower diagnostic thresholds on osteoporosis, diabetes, hypertension and high cholesterol.[132] The good intentions of professional societies to find and treat illness by lowering the threshold value for diagnosis opens the door wide to increased drug use.

HEALTHY REDEFINED OR WHO MOVED THE GOAL LINE?						
Osteoporosis in women	then	8,010,000	now	14,791,000	=	6,781,000 more sick people
High Blood Pressure	then	38,690,000	now	52,180,000	=	13,490,000 more sick people
High Cholesterol	then	49,480,000	now	92,127.000	=	42,647,000 more sick people
Diabetes	then	11,697,000	now	13,378,000	=	1,681,000 more sick people

By changing the definition of healthy, millions more are medicalized.

Being monitored for every little blip sucks us into a life and mindset that medicine is our god, our source, our only way. Assuming that every ache, or pain, or sad feeling is a sickness to be battled can cause us to believe that we are full of "abnormalities." We might even enjoy the tinkering physicians can do. Before we know it, we have capitulated to forces to which we are told we should submit.

With new definitions of high cholesterol, Big Pharma hit pay dirt. The first big drug for the management of cholesterol was Lipitor. It became available in 1996 and has been the top selling drug in the history of legal drugs with sales since 1996 exceeding $125 billion.[133] "In 2011, US doctors wrote nearly 250 million prescriptions for cholesterol-lowering drugs, creating a US $18.5-billion market," according to IMS Health, a healthcare technology and information company based in Danbury, Connecticut. "The drug industry in particular is very much in favor of target-based measures," says Joseph Drozda, a cardiologist and director of outcomes research at Mercy Health in Chesterfield, Missouri. "It drives the use of products."[134] The targets tend to change to include more and more people *needed* to hit the target!

Big Pharma's self-invented, target-based measures have enabled it to define the new "normal," and we take a pill to meet the definition. Fifteen years after people paid over $100 billion for Lipitor to get "normal," we read that Jay Cohn, a cardiologist at the University of Minnesota Medical School in Minneapolis, admitted that he "worries that the focus on LDL levels offers up the wrong patients for statin therapy. Most people who have a heart attack do not have high LDL. Cohn advocates treating patients with statins based on the state of health of their arteries, as revealed by non-invasive tests such as the ultrasound. "If your arteries and heart are healthy, I don't care what your LDL or blood pressures is,'" he says.[135]

Clearly, there is controversy on the statin topic.

WAKE UP AND LIVE ALL THE WAY TO THE END

Since birth, we have been lulled into living medicalized lives, and deep in our collective subconscious mind we expect some Christiaan Barnard or Peter Safar to save us from ourselves. But, history tells us this is not going to happen.

Remember typing college papers on a typewriter with carbon paper and long distance calls that cost so much you were only allowed to make them in a dire emergency? Medicine has changed as much or more than the ways we communicate and work, and those changes have kept death at bay. At the same time, our bodies keep pumping oxygen through their 60,000 miles of blood vessels and they are not the same as they used to be. Our bodies are machines and they exhibit wear and tear no matter what we do to find the fountain of youth. I wanted to be a bone marrow donor for the child of a dear friend and went to sign up but I'm too old. They only want donations from those who are eighteen to forty-four years of age.

Then there's just us. Science should not even try to save us from our poor choices. If we smoke too much, drink too much, eat too much, sit around too much, we have no one to blame when our doctor thinks it best to put us on blood pressure medicine. We have not taken personal responsibility and now we are going to fall at the feet of a physician and believe she can save us.

Shannon Brownlee says, "Think of doctors as guides, not gods."[136] We, the untrained and naive, have assigned more knowledge to medical science than it merits. Doctors know they do not have a cure for what happens to every human being. When we get sick, our hopeful innocence assumes that medicine has the cure, but sometimes we are wrong. It does not have a cure for what happens to every human being. To die gracefully and peacefully we must accept truth and even dig for truth.

The late, great physician Jeremy Swan was my friend. He was an internationally recognized cardiologist, scientist, researcher, innovator and teacher. With his colleague, Dr. William Ganz, he invented the Swan-Ganz catheter. He said to me, "Hattie, I'm a plumber. I have no idea why the body heals or how it really works. It's the work of our great God. Some just say it's a mystery."

Many of us grown-ups of the twenty-first century remember when we were told in junior high that we were going to the moon. We have done it, and accomplished so much more that it's no wonder a little thing like cancer seems easy to fix, and a little organ called the heart the size of a fist can be regulated—or replaced. These miracles don't change the fact that we still need to recognize what even the most well trained, respected and successful doctor knows: life is indeed still full of mysteries, and doctors can't solve every problem. In the end, they can't save themselves or us.

STEP 2 in taking control of end-of-life decisions is to recognize that medicine is too small when up against the force of nature. We are too trusting of medicine. Please answer the questions and fill in the blanks you will find on pages 192-196 of the MY WAY WORKBOOK.

4 STEPS
TO A
PEACEFUL
DEATH

---

1 ACKNOWLEDGE THE
INEVITABILITY OF DEATH

2 UNDERSTAND THE LIMITS
OF MEDICINE

3 EDUCATE YOURSELF ABOUT
YOUR HEALTHCARE CHOICES

4 COMMUNICATE YOUR WISHES
& CHOOSE A PROXY

CHAPTER 3

A GENTLE PATH

I n November of 2011 Dr. Ken Murray wrote about his friend, another physician, who was diagnosed with pancreatic cancer. That friend closed his office, never set foot in a doctor's office or a hospital again and enjoyed the last six months of his life at home with his family.[137] A retired clinical assistant professor of family medicine at the University of Southern California, Dr. Murray rarely went to hospitals for ten years before retirement because he did not want to be part of what his colleagues were doing there.

Another physician told me a similar story. She has a private practice taking care of patients who choose to wind down out of this life without the use of hospitals and aggressive or experimental treatments. She told me, "After thirty-seven years of working in hospitals I could not take it anymore. Most physicians I know do not know how to tell patients and families that death is coming and that the patient should be allowed to have a pain-free peaceful death. It's probably not about doctors wanting to make money by continuing to do treatments. It is about their egos—they just can't let a patient die. Some won't even write a DNR (do not resuscitate) order."

What precipitates this kind of response from physicians? Doctors know that breath is life and when it quits, we die. If everyone dies from lack of oxygen, does that mean death is simple?

HOW BREATHING STOPS

Many conditions can lead to our last breath, but there are a few basics worth knowing as we face the inevitability of our demise:

1. **Our heart stops**. The most common reason for this malfunction is that arteries clog and/or our body's electrical system goes haywire.

2. **Cancer takes over**. The American Cancer Society says that cancer is the general name for a group of more than one hundred diseases. As Dr. Nuland writes in *How We Die: Reflections on Life's Final Chapter*, "Cancer cells behave like the members of a barbarian horde run amok—leaderless and undirected but with a single-minded purpose: to plunder everything within reach...and they do not even have the decency to die when they should."[138] When we have more cancer cells than normal cells in our blood or an organ, our body capitulates to the barbarian horde.

3. **Lungs give up**. Chronic bronchitis, emphysema, pneumonia or fluid overload causes lungs to lose diffusion capacity and/or elasticity.

4. **Stroke**. Blood vessels in the brain become blocked by thrombosis (a blood clot in a blood vessel) or vessels break and bleed.

5. **Kidneys quit**. They slowly lose the ability to filter toxins.

6. **Livers fail, bones crumble and brains fall victim to tumors and inflammation and trauma**. Orthopedic surgeon, Dr. John Cazale told me, "The body is a machine and parts simply wear out over time."[139] Dr. Atul Gawande writes that there is no predictable path to our falling apart.[140] Internal medicine physician, Dr. Pat Gary said, "It is fairly straight forward. We all die of lack of oxygen whether it starts as blood loss from trauma, heart, lung or kidney disease, the end result is lack of oxygen to vital tissues. Those tissues die and so does the organism."[141]

If death is so simple, what could we possibly learn from doctors about dying well?

HARD DATA IS HARD TO FIND

Using the massive University of Southern California libraries, I can't find any physicians who have taken exception to Dr. Murray's conclusion and only a couple of journalists who questioned his results based on his lack of hard research.

British physician Martin Scurr also concurred with Dr. Murray. He wrote, "Most doctors like me would rather die than endure the pain of treatment we inflict on others for terminal diseases. Should I discover tomorrow that I have advanced life-threatening cancer, I won't go rushing to the doctors for a heavily invasive course of medical treatment. No, I will shut up my London surgery, head to my home in Norfolk, stock up on gin and tonic and have a jolly good time until I meet my end. Like most doctors, I understand that *much of what we offer patients who have serious, life-threatening illnesses is ultimately futile.*"[142]

Ann Neumann wrote an essay called, "Dying With Class," while taking care of a psychiatrist who was eighty and dying from lung cancer. In addition to quoting Dr. Murray's article about how doctors die, she herself says, "Doctors don't die the way the rest of us do. They know too much about the small return of aggressive treatment to put themselves through it. Doctors have witnessed enough to know how the end-of-life can go down. And they intimately know what a hospital environment is like; they get themselves out of it when they can, to go home for that final rest in their own beds."[143]

Carolyn McClanahan, a physician and financial planner who contributes to *Forbes Magazine*, linked to the article and fiercely defended Dr. Murray's lack of hard data. She went on to write, "To do a study on whether physicians die differently wouldn't be controlled, pass an ethics committee, or it would be picketed by the 'No, you can't go peacefully in the night' coalition. However, I can provide a small, informal study of the clients in my financial planning practice, most of whom are physicians. In my practice, not only do doctors plan to die differently, their families die differently also."[144, 145, 146]

Three surgeons refer to Dr. Murray's article then go on to say, "Surgeons, at some point, are patients, too. If surgeons evaluate themselves, what type and level of care would they prefer, particularly at the end-of-life? Many healthcare professionals and surgeons opt out of medical care in this situation. This decision may be surprising to the public, but not to most physicians. Many surgeons can recall a conversation regarding a critically ill, elderly patient lying on a proverbial mattress grave in the surgical intensive care unit (ICU) during which a physician or colleague has stated, 'Don't let that happen to me.'"[147]

Author of *Overtreated*, Shannon Brownlee defended Dr. Murray in her essay for *TIME*, "...there is good evidence that physicians have thought out end-of-life issues more thoroughly than laypeople and are more likely to decline medical intervention. For example, they sign advance directives far more often than the rest of us do."[148] Here she sends the reader to a study done by Dr. Joseph Gallo. Dr. Gallo shared his findings with me which showed that 64% of the physicians surveyed had advance directives[149] compared to 26.3%[150] of the general population.

Dr. Murray makes me wonder about the thoughts of the 850,000 American physicians. These are professionals who are molded and shaped by long years of study, scientific knowledge and skills that make them able to save people's lives. Physicians legitimately can and do take pride in their extraordinary service to mankind. And they have unique perspectives and knowledge on disease, dying, and death from which we can all learn.

Two physicians I interviewed told me a couple of the insider jokes. "Why are there nails in coffins? So the oncologists can't administer another chemo treatment." And, "Patient: Well Doc, how long do I have? Doc: Six months without chemo and six months with chemo that will feel like twenty-six months." While chemo treatments can be in the plan of the oncologist, going beyond a point that could produce a benefit is often demanded by the patient or the patient's family.

As these dark jokes reveal, treatment can be taken to a fault. Doctors who witness treatments on a regular basis know that for many patients, it can be a time of misery during which the patient may wish for death. Hospitalist Dr. Angelo Volandes writes, "...the overwhelming majority of us treat patients with serious illness in a manner we would never want for our loved ones, or even for ourselves."[151] Medicine is science and art and the art part comes to physicians after seeing hundreds and hundreds of cases. They know more than they can explain. They know there are some treatments they themselves will avoid.

In addition to asking doctors if they have an advance directive, Dr. Gallo and his colleagues asked doctors: "If you had brain damage or some brain disease that cannot be reversed and makes you unable to recognize people or speak understandably, but you have no terminal illness, and you live in this condition for a long time, indicate your wishes regarding the use of each of the following medical procedures."[152]

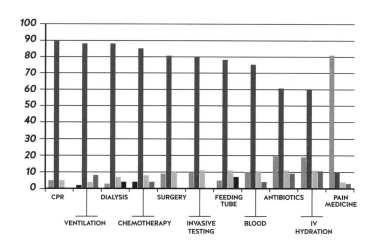

The results of this survey seem to corroborate Dr. Murray's article.

When I spoke with him on the phone, Dr. Gallo referred me to two more studies[153] he conducted with colleagues. These studies reveal that as physicians become frailer and perhaps suffer from depression, they might opt for what he calls a "higher burden of care."[154, 155, 156] Does this mean that at sixty years of age I am sure I do not want chemotherapy but at eighty I just might agree to it? Yes, we can all change our minds, and Dr. Gallo told me that these studies seem to indicate age might make us more tolerant to the inconveniences of being sick.

END-OF-LIFE GO-TO TREATMENTS

All the doctors that I've spoken with about end-of-life issues were very matter of fact in our discussions. Even though they are talking about their own death, they are calm, practical, rational and even stoic. Most physicians see extraordinary life-saving treatments as somewhat useful but only on a temporary basis. Here are comments made to me by physicians I interviewed over a two-year period about these common treatments *if they were given the option to use for themselves*:

CPR: "futile, odds aren't good"

VENTILATION: "no hole cut in throat but could intubate for a few days"

DIALYSIS: "chronic malaise, fatigue, nausea, blood pressure going up and down"

CHEMOTHERAPY: "vomiting, weakness and it doesn't always work; question everything"

SURGERY: "I'd rather not; need to know the purpose; the stats"

INVASIVE TESTING: "from surgery to drawing blood; depends"

FEEDING TUBE: "not for me"

BLOOD: "maybe one transfusion, but no more; do not want to depend upon it having to be repeated"

ANTIBIOTICS: "if I am comatose or have lost my mind and I get an infection just kiss me goodbye"

IV HYDRATION: "no thanks unless it's just to get me over a non-serious illness"

It seems to me that all of these treatments put us in a state of helplessness and while physicians might expect the rest of us to accept this, they do not want to be helpless. They know the risk versus the benefits of each. I am learning that they question everything while the rest of us might just go along to get along. We might just assume that if something is being done to us this is best. My mom's story taught me that I want to question everything.

Looking to discover if physicians have changed their attitudes about advance directives and their own end-of-life care since Dr. Gallo's study, Dr. Vyjeyanthi Periyakoil and colleagues asked 1,147 physicians to answer fourteen questions. The results, titled "Do Unto Others," reveal a disconnect between what doctors recommend to their patients and what they would want for themselves. Dr. Peryakoil writes, "It is likely that doctors recurrently witness the tremendous suffering their terminally ill patients experience as they undergo ineffective, high intensity treatments at the end-of-life and they (the doctors) consequentially wish to forego such treatments for themselves."[157]

MY PERSONAL QUEST TO UNDERSTAND

In preparation for attending two large (1,000 attendees each) national meetings for physicians specializing in the field of palliative medicine (these physicians take advanced training to be board certified in palliative medicine in addition to their primary practice), I prepared a simple, non-scientific and informal questionnaire to ascertain how doctors would want to live out their last days if suffering from a terminal illness. The background information I gathered from each respondent included:

- Name
- Medical specialty
- Year graduated from medical school
- Current medical directive—yes or no
- Designated proxy, if applicable
- Relationship of proxy to them and if that person
  was a healthcare professional

The actual choices for "how I want to die" were

- In my sleep
- At home
- In ICU
- In hospice
- Fast and painless
- I want to do everything possible to stay alive

Again, while my survey was not scientific, I gained some interesting insights from the one hundred doctors who responded.

- Not one physician chose "ICU/hospital" or "Do everything possible." None chose "In my sleep."
- 85% chose "at home surrounded by my friends and family."
- 15% (all male and young docs) say they want to die in a manner that is "fast and painless."
- Several said they wanted to check out while doing the thing they love—such as playing a fast game of basketball, winning the game and then dropping dead while running off the court.
- A couple of others chose a more adventurous ending. One said he wanted to die mountain climbing; while a difficult diagnosis for another was the signal to his daughter to buy a one-way ticket for him and a two-way ticket for her so that he can lie on a beach in the Caribbean, watch the water and feel the heat. He said he would stop eating and drinking and the heat would move him to death faster.
- Several physicians spoke from a treatment-specific perspective. One physician who works with burn victims told her husband—who is also a physician—that if she ever suffers burns over more than 25% of her body, the only treatment she wants is palliative care. Her overall goal would be to improve her and her family's quality of life while she is ill.
- Two young physicians who work in the ICU in a busy New York City hospital told me they forbid that anyone cut a hole in their throat for a ventilator or a hole in their stomach for a feeding tube.

- With a big smile on his face, Dr. Gallo told me he wants to die the way his father died. He said, "My father was not big on medicine. He died at home surrounded by family."
- One physician said he would very much like to die at home and he would like about six weeks so he could say goodbye to his many friends. He added, "I won't need hospice. I am hospice."
- Two physicians told me the functional clues that would tell their families when to stop curative care and move to comfort care only. One said, "When I poop and pee in my bed" and the other said, "When I can't wipe my backside." I asked the ER doctor who said this why her directive is worded this way and she said, "If I can't wipe my backside means that either my brain is not able to send instructions or I am no longer able to use my hands. While some people can be happy in this situation, the use of my mind and my hands is very important to me and without them the quality of my life would be so poor I would simply be ready to let go of this life."
- Finally, one doctor, born in 1950, said he'd agree to a stay in ICU with intubation for breathing for a couple of days, but no incision in his throat. This matches up with Dr. Gallo's findings that some physicians would accept a trial period for "keeping them alive."

No physician, in this survey or in any interview, has told me that they want to linger for years.

Physician, oncologist, policy adviser and bioethicist, Ezekiel Emanuel, says he hopes he (and all the rest of us) will die at or before the age of seventy-five. He writes that at seventy-five and beyond, "I won't actively end my life. But I won't try to prolong it, either…I will stop getting any regular preventive tests and I will accept only palliative—not curative—treatment if I am suffering pain or other disability….After seventy-five, if I develop cancer, I will refuse treatment. Similarly, no cardiac stress test. No pacemaker and certainly no implantable defibrillator. No heart-valve replacement or bypass surgery….Flu shots are out….and no to antibiotics." He goes on, "Obviously, a do-not-resuscitate order and a complete advance directive indicating no ventilators, dialysis, surgery, antibiotics, or any other medication—nothing except palliative care."[158]

In her book, physician Jeanne Fitzpatrick has a simple form for providing instructions to our selected proxy and our physician. In addition she says, "If I descend into dementia and for six months do not recognize friends or family members, provide only comfort care. No resuscitation, no antibiotics, stop all usual medicine, no food or water unless I choose it or request it, and no intravenous fluids or feeding tubes."[159]

These are only a few examples of how physicians want their lives to play out in the end. And I gathered these comments by asking, "How do you want to die?" This is personal and I only give these examples as they provide clear direction to their families and friends which is what you each want to provide as you answer the questions in the workbook for yourself.

MIRACLES

Now here's a shocking study conclusion: doctors don't believe in miracles to the same degree as the general public.

> More of the public (57.4 %) than the professionals (19.5%) believe that divine intervention could save a person when physicians believe treatment is futile.[160]

This may be another reason that many doctors don't keep pushing for more treatments for themselves. They understand their body, the prognosis for their illness, take some practical treatments, and then know when to say no more. My surgeon neighbor told me about his fifty-year-old colleague who was diagnosed with one of the blood cancers. That doctor told my neighbor, "It blows my mind that in one year from now, I'll be dead." And, he was right. He tried the treatment available and knew it would not work.

Another surgeon told me, "When I tell a family that I have done everything I can do, so many times they say to me, 'Doctor, surely you have a miracle in your back pocket.' I have to tell them, 'No doctor has miracles to give, only expertise and skill. And I have given you all that I have that is mine to give.'"[161]

The upside of being a physician is they know a lot about disease; the downside is they know a lot about disease. Doctors are not so good at fooling themselves and at the same time they are careful not to discourage their patients. We all know that hope is powerful and is needed by the patient if they are to recover from some difficult disease or accident. If you want to fight against a physical problem, you will want a physician who will help you by keeping your hope alive.

GO TO THE MOVIES

The old adage is that a picture is worth a thousand words. What I see happening in real time or what I see captured in high definition video can explain a complex idea quicker and have more impact than if I only read about it. This, to me, is the huge advantage physicians and nurses have when it comes to achieving a peaceful death. I imagine them swimming in the sea of heroic treatments, seeing drugs and technology in vivid color until their patients are cast in the starring role. Then, no matter how hard the patients swim or how much oxygen they have left in their tank, sometimes the killer shark called "the disease" catches up to them and puts an end to their life.

Harvard Medical School is trying to help laypersons understand what treatments are actually like so we can decide if we want them or not. Physician, professor, author, filmmaker and cofounder of Advanced Care Planning Decisions, Angelo Volandes, has made simple, short films about some procedures and conditions we laypeople don't understand. While attending a seminar recently, I watched the film about CPR. Even as a healthy sixty-five year-old, I didn't like what I saw and I really don't want that "life-saving" treatment done to me. I would rather go out in a short blast of pain that stops my breath than have a machine attached to me that sends shocks to an already damaged heart. There is no law that requires me to receive that or any other type of treatment.

Dr. Volandes is convinced that his films can change how we think about end-of-life care and I am 100% on his side. His organization is a nonprofit foundation developing and researching video decision support tools and making them available to the healthcare community. Currently thirty-five health systems are using the organization's videos as part of their standard of care for patients with advanced diseases.[162] On his website, Dr. Volandes explains why he is making this information widely available.[163]

Ask your physician if he owns a library of Advanced Care Planning Decision films. If not, encourage him to purchase them, or find out if he knows where you could obtain them. These films will help you become more informed about the treatment choices available and make better decisions about what you would accept or not accept in an emergency or as you age and become sicker and frail.

COMPLETE AND HONEST COMMUNICATION

"The Charter on Medical Professionalism" was first published in 2002 and since then it has been endorsed by at least one hundred professional groups and is used in medical education. It sets out a list of profession-al responsibilities, and one of those is a commitment to honesty with patients. "Physicians must ensure that patients are completely and hon-estly informed before the patient has consented to treatment and after treatment has occurred. This expectation does not mean that patients should be involved in every minute decision about medical care; rather, they must be empowered to decide on the course of therapy."[164]

Ten years after the charter had gained wide acceptance, 1,891 phy-sicians responded to a survey conducted to learn if physicians were actually living up to the charter. The results revealed that in the area of honesty with patients, "more than half said that they had described a prognosis more positively than the facts warranted."[165] This must be the reason why, "A recent study found that around 70% to 80% of patients with a poor prognosis incorrectly believed that their treatments were likely to result in a cure."[166] While patients are regularly unaware of the reality of the future, doctors understand the full scope of a prognosis. Geriatrician Dr. Daniel Matlock told me, "No one is going to maintain my false hope."[167]

This seems to be another reason doctors approach their own deaths differently than the rest of us. Certainly, doctors don't try to pull the wool over the eyes of another doctor. They speak the same language and understand prognoses in a way laypeople do not. Doctors feel sure that their fellow doctor can take the raw data; bad news doesn't have to be couched in soft language or spun to sound upbeat.

In her blog, Maggie Mahar references Clifton Leaf's book, *The Truth in Small Doses: Why We're Losing the War on Cancer—and How to Win It*, by saying that when people talk about the successful war on cancer, "they greatly exaggerate our success. When it comes to breast cancer, for example, 30 years after we launched the war, the number of women per 100,000 who die of breast cancer had actually grown from 28.4 per 100,000 in 1970 to 29.2 per 100,000 in 2000."[168]

Writing for *CNN Money* in 2004, Leaf points out that we are not winning the war on cancer. "Thirty-three years ago, fully half of cancer patients survived five years or more after diagnosis. The figure has crept up to about 63% today...long-term survival for advanced cancer has barely budged since the 1970s."[169] In the same book, Leaf lays out some hard-to-swallow facts. In a *Wall Street Journal* review, Leaf points out that $300 billion has been spent since President Nixon launched the war on cancer in 1971.

> Though cancer death rates are on the decline in the US, the data is misleading, Mr. Leaf shows, and depends on whether the rates are age-adjusted. The raw numbers are still daunting: The most recent show 1.6 million new cases and nearly 600,000 deaths in 2012. While 67% of newly diagnosed cancer patients are expected to "survive," that only means that they are alive five years after their diagnosis; fewer than a fifth of patients with cancers of the lung, pancreas, liver or esophagus are expected to live that long. New therapies such as Avastin, Herceptin and Gleevec—which treat colon cancer, breast cancer and a form of leukemia, respectively—have proved successful in many patients, but resistance often emerges and cancer returns.[170]

Doctors know this. And they know the data about all the other things that will kill us. When a sick doctor is presented with the facts of his or her disease, the sick doctor understands it. We are often not given the same facts and would not interpret them in the same way as a medical professional. If we do figure it out, it would be after we have sloughed through the inconveniences of being a patient for months or years. Doctors know a great deal about the reasons we die and what treatments do and don't work.[171] So why can't they just tell us this stuff?

Here's what I think:

- They are rushed by the system.
- It's difficult for them to put into words what they know innately.
- They actually think you know more than you know.
- They learned the language of medicine in medical school and it's hard for them to speak without using it so they actually do tell us but we don't get it.
- They forgot what it was like not to know what they know.
- Many do not think of death as part of their work. They don't want to look at your case that way.
- In 1982, Medicare set up a separate benefit called hospice and most doctors have nothing to do with it and don't want to have anything to do with it. They trust the forward march of medicine and want to see new treatments tested.
- Doctors don't like the idea that their patient is dying any more than the patient does. It's a difficult discussion all around.
- Primary care doctors know that they will be sending you to a specialist.
- Doctors went to medical school to heal people.
- They have not been taught how to discuss end-of-life with patients so they can't practice what they don't know.

Now, knowing this with these possibilities in mind, we have to learn to communicate and partner with our doctors so they tell us what we need to know so that we can live the life we want to live and maximize our chance of dying gently. It is not our doctor's job to live our life, it is *our* job. We must strap on our courage, take our brains out of neutral and get ready for this to happen. When we or a loved one gets a difficult diagnosis, we must make sure the conversation includes our desires as a patient.

The doctor says: "You have stage 4 breast cancer." (Or, you fill in the diagnosis.) Tough conversations go better with practice, practice, practice. Listen to yourself, say the words, then practice again. Here are a couple of approaches that illustrate what you might say:

1. "What you said the other day doesn't sound good, and I have to get used to the idea. Sounds like this could kill me sooner than later. Do I need to start giving my furniture away? (Or, you can say something else that might lighten the moment.) For now, let's fill in a POLST (Physicians Orders for Life Sustaining Treatment) and let's make sure you have my advance directive and the contact information for my proxy."

   (Turn to pages 139-140 to see a sample POLST. Your doctor will have the right one for the state you live in. Ask for a copy of what you fill in with the doctor then tape it in the back of this book. When you get really sick, get another copy from your doctor and tape it to your refrigerator door. The POLST for the state I live in is bright orange and some are pink. This is so it can be spotted quickly on your refrigerator if the 911 team shows up to get you.)

2. "This is too much for me to take in right now. I'll come back with my husband (or a friend) and a recording device when you can see me in a couple of days. Do you have anything I can read or a website you would recommend where I can learn more before I see you again? Heads up: I want the truth, unvarnished. I want worst-case scenario and best-case. Don't worry, I can take it. I want to know the historical trajectory of this disease. I want to know your one-year plan, three-year plan and five-year plan."

3. "Do you have any patients you are treating for this now who would be willing to talk with me? I realize that you can't give me those names and numbers without getting their permission so maybe you can check with them and have some names when I come back."

4. "I want to work with a palliative team as I work with you. I want you to arrange for me to meet with a nurse or physician on that team after you have given me your ideas." (Please turn to page 149 in the glossary for a full definition of Palliative Medicine.)

5. "My primary concern is how I live my days, the quality of my life. I know I am aging and will never be thirty or forty or fifty again. I am ready to do all of this thoughtfully and gracefully even when it means that my body is going to quit and I die."

Doctors don't want to scare you or bring up words like "terminal" or "death" or phrases like "this can/may/will kill you." Now that you have brought it up, the conversation is yours to lead. Most doctors will happily follow your lead to answer your questions. They don't want to be vague; however, they have learned from experience that patients receiving news of a bad prognosis don't, won't, or can't hear the straightforward, unvarnished truth.

Doctors have learned to give us time-released truth, but if you take charge, you can get as much as you can take in at that moment.[172] Generally, a tiny dose of information is given, then we go home and come back and we get another tiny dose then we go home and get another tiny dose and by that time, we might be dead.

But, it is from *us* that doctors have learned that they can't say the words "terminal" or "fatal" because those words cause our hearing to fail. Our emotions take over and we zoom off to movies in our minds of grandchildren we won't see graduate from college, the Christmas dinner without you at the head of the table or the kids out fishing and falling in because you aren't there to tell them to be careful. This is the reason doctors don't say those words: we won't hear them.

WORDS DON'T MEAN THE SAME THING

When you arrive for the next discussion with your doctor, do not assume that you will understand one word the doctor says.[173] While they speak English, they speak it as it is used and taught in medical school.[174]

They say: **Acute**

You think: Serious, will kill me.	They think: This just popped up; it is not chronic.

They say: **Treatment**

You think: Cure.	They think: process/procedure/protocol/usual intervention.

They say: **Adverse drug reaction**

You think: I'll get a rash.	They think: you could end up dead/in the hospital/this has a wide range of meanings, can run the gamut; no intent to indicate severity only thinking of the cause.

They say: **Perhaps**

You think: Of course.

They think: maybe but more likely not.

They say: **We can try**

You think: It will work.

They think: It is technically possible to do this but there is no suggestion of success.

They say: **We can enroll you in a study**

You think: Great. I'm going to get cutting-edge treatment!

They think: You fit the criteria we are seeking for the research. You want to participate in order to add to medical knowledge.

They say: **We know a little**

You think: They know more than they are telling me.

They think: This is totally experimental with no proven long-term positive results.

They say: **Adjuvant therapy**

You think: I have no idea.

They think: What we'll do after we have done surgery chemotherapy and/or radiation.

They say: **Your cancer has responded to the chemotherapy**

You think: I am going to be cured.

They think: There has been some effect on the tumor.

Often, you can ask the nurses on the team for more information. They can interpret or review the discussion with you. They know the team and are familiar with how the team works.

Dr. Susan Block is an important person in the field of palliative care. She is professor of psychiatry at Harvard Medical School and she is trying to teach physicians how to engage in conversations with patients who have less than a year to live. She has developed the "Serious Illness Communications List" and will teach physicians and nurses how to use it. Here's what she wants the doctor to learn from the patient:

- Their understanding of the prognosis.[175]
- How much information they want shared with loved ones.
- Their goals of care, should their health seriously worsen.
- Their biggest fears and what functional abilities they could not imagine living without.
- How much medical intervention they are willing to undergo to gain more time.
- How much they want family members to know about their priorities and wishes.[176]

What you should be asking yourself at this point is *why does my doctor have to ask me this?* And, what you should be thinking is *I need to be telling my doctor these things.* If we want to die gently, as many doctors seek to do for themselves, we have to be a patient like a doctor would be a patient. While all of us want some form of warmth extended to us, if you demand coddling you may never get to the truth. I imagine that when a doctor delivers a serious diagnosis to another doctor, there is no coddling going on.

YOU ARE BACK FOR MORE

You heard a serious diagnosis from your doctor a few days ago, and now you are back with one or two companions, a recording device, a notepad and pen. Sit in a chair as close as you can to the doctor, and remember, doctors have lots and lots of information to give you, but it is not necessarily advice. Remember that you are the "customer;" you are the one buying and receiving treatment. Don't be afraid to ask questions. One study shows that we don't want to ask questions as we see the physician as the authority and don't want to be "difficult."[177]

According to 2014 data, the majority of US doctors spend between 13 to 20 minutes per patient. This is not a lot of time when you need to speak about life and death matters, so your preparation going into that appointment is key.[178] Take a look at the following two scenarios and imagine yourself in the role of the patient.

SCENARIO ONE

DOCTOR: "So, Mrs. Jones, I saw your blood work that was drawn two days ago. Nothing has changed. Your blood pressure is good—so is your potassium and sodium. I know you stated the other day that you don't want to come to the clinic often and you want to avoid the ER and the ICU. But, you have a very serious illness and I am equipped to help you. If you want to live as long as possible, you have to go through chemotherapy every three weeks. After that, we will have to do radiation. We will have to monitor you closely. I know you want to be in control, but right now, your cancer is in control and I can help you get back in control soon."

PATIENT: "Well, I am more concerned about quality of life. Taking chemotherapy every three weeks and coming in to get my blood work drawn and getting x-rays sounds exhausting. We live sixty-five miles away from here. My husband is on disability and it would be almost impossible for me to make all of these trips. I don't want to spend what little time I have left taking these trips. It sounds very futile to me. I want to save my energy to be with my family and friends."

DOCTOR: "I am afraid that you do not fully understand how ill you are."

PATIENT: "Doctor, will I survive this stage 4, very aggressive tumor? Will I be alive in 1 year?"

DOCTOR: "Well, I'm not God, so I can't really say."

PATIENT: "How many patients like me have you cared for that died within the year of being diagnosed with this type of cancer?"

DOCTOR: "This is a difficult question because every patient is different. But, I am confident I can help slow the cancer down and give you more time here with the chemotherapy."

PATIENT: "Do you have patients who have gone through this treatment regime and have lived longer than patients who have not?"

DOCTOR: "That's hard to say."

PATIENT: "I imagine I will not be able to drive myself home from a treatment, correct?"

DOCTOR: "Yes, you will not be able to drive, because we will give you medicine at the beginning of the chemotherapy that will make you a little sleepy."

PATIENT: "I have insurance but I am wondering if you have any idea what my insurance might not pay? What are the costs of being sick like this? Of course there is the cost of driving and someone taking time off of work to go back and forth with me. "

DOCTOR: "Yes, I have a staff member who deals with insurance companies. She can help you as you leave today."

PATIENT: "I do want to be responsible about finances. I don't want to spend money on treatments that will be futile and decrease the quality of life I have left. Why should I spend money we really don't have or dip into savings that my family can use in the future? Maybe my husband and I would like to dip into our savings to go to Patagonia, which is one of the places on my travel-to list. Then when I'm gone, he'll still have savings to go on more trips."

DOCTOR: "We will work with your insurance company and make sure you know exactly what will be covered by them and what will not. "

HUSBAND: "Look, everyone needs to know that I will do whatever my wife wants. I can try to do the driving, but is it fair for all of us to pressure her to suffer? We have talked about the day when one of us will hear a hard-to-hear truth. She does not want to compromise the time we have left together. Am I right sweetheart?"

PATIENT: "Right. Treatment doesn't sound like good quality of life for me. It's not going to buy me any more time—if anything it will complicate my life with appointments, being sick with the chemotherapy, etc. As I mentioned the other day, I want to have a palliative care consult to assist with my pain and other symptoms. I would like to begin with a palliative care consultation next week."[179]

DOCTOR: "Well, I don't think you need palliative care at this point."

PATIENT: "I am making a request of you, as my doctor. I want a palliative care consult."

DOCTOR: "OK. Let me see what I can do."

Your doctor may not quickly agree to send you to another physician. Your doctor may hope that you will agree to let them do what they do best; however, that may not be what is best for you. This is your decision. This is the one area you do have control over.

SCENARIO TWO

DOCTOR: "I am glad we can have this conversation today. Before I forget, you had asked if you could speak with one of my patients who had the same diagnosis. We have gotten in touch with Susan—she was diagnosed with the same disease three months ago. Both she and her husband are open to speaking with you, as well as your husband, if you would like. I will give you her phone number before you leave."

"You made it clear the other day that you want me to be open and honest with you. That is my intention. While I went to medical school to 'heal,' it is always difficult to have to give devastating news to patients, as I had to give to you two days ago. While we cannot heal your disease, we can provide you with good care for both you and your family. We are committed to providing you the best care possible."

PATIENT: "I have done some research in the past couple of days on my disease and I know this is very serious. Ten years ago I completed an advanced directive and I am still committed to those same thoughts today. I want to die at home, with my family around me. I want to avoid hospitals—especially the ER and the ICU. My main questions revolve around pain management. Who will oversee that? What about my breathlessness? My fatigue? My anxiety? I don't want to drive into town every week to visit a doctor. I don't want to put my family through that. How do I talk to my family? They are hurting now. I have some financial issues that I need to take care of before I die. When should I do that? I want to say 'good-bye' to my family well. How do I go about that?"

DOCTOR: "These are all excellent questions and I can tell you have been doing lots of thinking over these past 48 hours. I will still be your physician and will monitor your pain and other symptoms. It's not unusual for you to be anxious—you have received some very bad news. I can give you some medication for that. I know you don't want to drive into town, but we will need to monitor your blood counts and do x-rays from time to time. Yes, you may have a difficult time breathing and you will want to come to the ER. That's not unusual. But, we will set you up with oxygen in your home and hopefully your shortness of breath will not be too bad." "I know this is a difficult time for you and your family. Just take each day as it comes—make the most of each day. I am glad to hear that you have completed your advanced directive—that is very helpful."

"So, I do need to see you again in a couple of weeks. Here is a lab requisition for a blood drawn and a chest x-ray. Please make sure to do these at least two days before our next appointment so we can discuss results."

PATIENT: "No. I don't want to do all of this. I don't want to come into town for these visits. I want palliative care. I want you to connect me with the palliative care team."

DOCTOR: "OK. I know the team well and they will be able to work with me as we pay attention to your pain and symptoms. I will call the team now."

Dr. Richard Della Penna warns that physicians resist inviting palliative teams to join a case. He says, "Physicians working in hospitals are overly focused on the details and don't think about the whole person; they are taught to be loners and don't really want to play on a team; they don't want to take time to deal with another physician, a nurse, a social worker and a chaplain; and, they simply don't communicate well. So the end result is, they don't speak much and keep working on the part of the person which demands their particular expertise. Thus, the seriously ill person and their families often never even learn about the benefits of palliative care." He adds, "Do not expect your physician to do what you want. They tend to do what they want to do."[180]

It is up to you to do what the doctor suggests—all of it, some of it, or none of it. You can follow the recommended treatment plan or go home and never walk into a provider's office or hospital again. If you decide that you do not want treatment, tell the doctor that you simply want the palliative care team to take your case. My friend's ninety-year-old mom did just that and lived for four more years.

RESPECTING FINAL WISHES

Now it happens. You age, get frail, your brain gets fuzzy and you can't toilet by yourself. You gasp for breath one day and someone calls 911. Everything you wrote down is ignored because a family member has his or her own emotional/psychological/spiritual problem with letting you die or they have never seen your directive because you didn't show it to everyone you know. Your wishes go missing, like the story I heard about one man's will that was cut into tiny pieces then flushed down the toilet by his daughter. Children who don't like what you wrote in your directive or your will can destroy it if others let them get away with it.

We need to ensure that our families will respect our final wishes. A strong surrogate, which I will explain in Chapter 4, seems to be the best way to getting close to this goal.

Doctors know what their own colleague, Dr. Sherwin Nuland, wrote so beautifully:

> Each disease is a distinctive process—it carries its own particular kind of destructive work within a framework of highly specific patterns. When we are familiar with the patterns of the illness that afflicts us, we disarm our imaginings. Accurate knowledge of how a disease kills serves to free us from unnecessary terrors of what we might be fated to endure when we die. We may thus be better prepared to recognize the stations at which it is appropriate to ask for relief, or perhaps to begin contemplating whether to end the journey altogether.[181]

In 2014, Dr. Nuland died at the age of eight-two at home surrounded by his family.

STEP 3 in taking control of end-of-life decisions is learning that you have choices. You are not required to passively delegate death to a system that insists upon surgery, stents, chemotherapy, blood transfusions, radiation, infusions and all of the tubes, bags and lines which accompany these interventions. Please answer the questions and fill in the blanks you will find on pages 197-201 of the MY WAY WORKBOOK.

4 STEPS
TO A
PEACEFUL
DEATH

---

1 ACKNOWLEDGE THE
INEVITABILITY OF DEATH
2 UNDERSTAND THE LIMITS
OF MEDICINE
3 EDUCATE YOURSELF ABOUT
YOUR HEALTHCARE CHOICES
4 COMMUNICATE YOUR
WISHES & CHOOSE A PROXY

CHAPTER 4

CREATE YOUR CIRCLE OF CARE

"Take control. Don't be passive. Clarify for yourself and your family what you hope for in the future when you become ill or frail. Gather the courage to have hard conversations. If you want meaning all the way to the end and a peaceful, natural death, you'll need to work to make it happen. Decide before you become ill or frail that you want meaning all the way to the end."
– *Dr. Laura Morrison*[182]

In 1998, Margaret Edson's play, *Wit*, depicted the heart-rending, but all too common, tale of a woman dying of ovarian cancer. She had no family and didn't invite friends to support her through her illness and the treatments that ensued. She agreed to participate in a clinical trial, and other than one compassionate nurse, she lay in her bed on a near-empty stage all alone, day after day. It was a clear example of art imitating life. While we can pretend this play was merely macabre artistic expression, deep down we know that this happens all too frequently.

In 2012, Best Picture-nominated French film *Amour* told the story of an elderly couple in the throes of end-of-life crisis. When the wife's surgery to unblock a carotid artery goes wrong, leaving her paralyzed on her right side and confined to a wheelchair, she begs her husband to promise he will never take her back to the hospital ever again. Her husband bears the burden of responsibility of her care alone. While *Wit* was about death in a sterile environment devoid of family or friends, *Amour* exposes us to 127 minutes under the weight of the husband's loving struggle to take care of his beloved wife, including his own stress-induced death no doubt accelerated by the promise he made to her and kept.

Neither of these artistic interpretations paints a very pretty picture of life for the person with a major life-changing, life-limiting, incurable condition. Unfortunately, these scenarios and potentially worse become more and more likely as the demographics and dynamics of our culture undergo radical change.

THE CHANGING AMERICAN FAMILY

One of the biggest problems with getting sick or growing old in America today is that family relationships are more complex than ever. Some families may rise to the occasion, while some are falling apart and far-flung. At the same time, modern medicine has layered complexity upon complexity to the treatment of illness. If you are in your fifties, sixties or seventies, you may remember a grandparent (or even a parent) dying in their (or even your) home. Home is where people *used* to go to die surrounded by the family they had cared for and who now cared for them. Those were the days when there might be a family member home to help, but now most adults are working at least forty hours a week. And those were the days before we had treatments, let alone cures, for the most common diseases that robbed past generations of long, long lives. It was before we had multi-million dollar facilities to house multi-million dollar equipment designed to discover or treat disease. In the old days, hardening of the arteries (arteriosclerosis) was a death sentence, consumption (tuberculosis) quarantined you to a hot, dry climate—if you could afford it—and dropsy (edema or swelling due to fluid retention) was caused by any host of underlying diseases—hopefully, one that didn't kill you.

Medicine and disease are no longer as predictable or as personal as they used to be. Thanks to the exponential growth of disease understanding and advancements in biomedical technology in just the past fifty years, people today are definitely living longer, on average, than our ancestors did. The downside is that we can expect our loved ones to be with us longer—but not necessarily in the way they want to be or the way we may want them to be. Caring for those with chronic illness or those dying extracts a heavy toll on the family and friends[183] who care for the sick person. Medicine has made it possible to treat disease and prolong life, but toward the very end, family and friends too often are only the helpless bystanders or crazed advocates.

Like it or not, just as generations before us have, as we age we will become il and we will need a support system which is made up of family, close friends, neighbors and medical professionals. The expectation of professional twenty-four-hour care is both unrealistic and cost prohibitive, and the personal toll on families, spouses or significant others extracts precious human energy at a time when it is most needed. You can't expect the professionals to do it all, nor family, spouse or significant other. Both approaches will disappoint. Without family and friends, we are dependent on institutional help. Conversely, if we don't engage professionals, our friends and family can be crushed under the burden.[184]

Running counter to this need for engagement at this most vulnerable time in our lives is the fact that more and more people in the US live alone. The US Census Bureau's data collected in the spring of 2012 reported that, "The proportion of one-person households increased by 10 percentage points between 1970 and 2012, from 17% to 27%."[185] This trend is even more pronounced among women. A 2011 report by the US Administration on Aging shows that nearly half of women over seventy-five live alone.[186]

In the United States, living alone is not considered to be negative and many seem to enjoy the personal freedom. We can live alone and during illness our biological family is replaced by paid professionals working for some part of the modern medical community or those who clean, cook and run errands. Medical care is paid for by Medicare, but most custodial care is paid for out of our pockets. What many seniors strive to do is avoid burdening anyone[187] they care about. The only option is to go to a healthcare provider alone and pretend to everyone else that everything in our life is smooth and that we are still in control. As seniors, we don't want anyone to even know that we had trouble passing the vision test when we went to renew our driver's license.

HOSPITALIZATION: FRIEND OR FOE?

The likelihood that we will one day need a hospital is increasing as we continue to live longer, many of us with chronic illness. It turns out that our confidence in the hospital as a place of healing may be misplaced. In fact, the hospital may be the *last* place we want to be. Dr. Harlan Krumholz says:

> In the hospital, in the course of being treated for the acute illness, people are sleep deprived, malnourished, deconditioned, disrupted in their routines, have their circadian rhythms jarred, medicated with drugs that affect judgment and function, and so on. The focus is on acute care and life-saving therapies, but in the course of doing good we are stressing patients in all sorts of ways. And it is not just physical stress, but emotional and social stress, too. All these challenges that patients endure during their acute treatment may affect health in the period that follows.[188]

For many seniors, a hospital admission incurs more negative than positive outcomes. According to one study, delirium or acute confusion, is a frequent visitor of the aged and is the most common complication of hospitalization among people ages sixty-five and over: 20% of those admitted to hospitals, up to 60% of those who have certain surgeries, and almost 80% of those treated in ICUs develop delirium.

Harvard Women's Health Watch reports, "Anything that interrupts normal brain function can cause delirium.... In vulnerable individuals, delirium can be induced by infection, insufficient food and drink, a trauma such as surgery or injury, uncontrolled pain, medications that most people tolerate well, or simply the unfamiliar surroundings of a hospital."[189] When delirium goes unrecognized, it can hinder recovery. Prolonged delirium is associated with poor long-term outcomes (mental and physical) and a higher mortality rate.[190] Consider what ICU physician William Silvester writes, "About 85% of us die after a chronic illness like dementia and up to half of us are not in a position to make our own decisions when we are close to death."[191] Moreover, these adverse events that happen in the month after the hospitalization are not directly related to the initial reason for hospitalization in the first place.

So, despite the evidence that the antiseptic cocoon of the hospital more often than not results in discomfort for the patient, family members tend to feel that their loved one is safer in a hospital than they are at home. The good side of this is that the family may care and want the best; the dark side is that the family doesn't know how to care for their loved one, even if they wanted to handle the illness—let alone the emotional messiness so often involved when those we love get sick.

A CAUTIONARY TALE

While the above discussion is not intended to scare anyone away from seeking the treatment needed when illness strikes, an over-reliance or dependence on the current healthcare system can easily and unwittingly lead us to think that modern medicine is all we need to live and die as we wish. Even in an out-patient clinic, we can feel as if we are the center of some very important universe. Blood is drawn, digital images are taken and a group—not just one person—of very smart people hover over us and our data. Our data is entered into the electronic health records to be shared by all who might need to be part of our treatment. Present ourselves with an ache or pain, and the entire system, starting with our primary care doctor, springs into action to save us. Actually the medical system is at the center and we are just passing through.

Medicine is just fine if you have the flu, but as we age and get sicker and sicker things change. While many tests and procedures have a legitimate place in diagnosing and treating illness, doctors may order tests and procedures because a patient has read about certain things and requests them, or the doctor is playing it safe to avoid litigation or there are pathways to care that dictate them.[192, 193] No one asks if treatment will be altered because of it, or if the treatment affects quality of life. Dr. Gary told me that she can most often diagnose a problem without imaging technology, but a patient with generous insurance might say to her, "Aren't you going to order an MRI?" At that point, she might acquiesce to the request out of respect for the patient but not because she believes she will see something that she had not already figured out.[194]

Research funded by Compassion & Choices revealed that twenty-five million Americans have received excessive or unwanted medical treatment.[195] This might show that even when a patient is ready to stop receiving particular types of treatments, the medical professionals keep providing them. Dr. Elizabeth Chaitin has worked in a hospital setting for nearly three decades and believes that when it comes to illness, physicians have a "hope that keeps hoping. They want to see their patients get well."

CRUNCH POINT

What happens, however, when we get a difficult diagnosis? When all that our marvelous medical system has to offer, short of a miracle, has been tried and we face the tough question of what next and the answer is, "There is nothing more we can do for you"[196] Dr. Charles von Gunten, oncologist and palliative care physician, says that 10% to 30% of patients with cancer do not want to make the choices.[197] He says this group of patients wants the oncologist to set out the plan for their care. The problems come where there is no advance directive, the professionals proceed with treatments with expected benefits.

The questions we face at that point are much more difficult and require soul-searching—and the support of those around us. How are you going to die? Where will you be when you die? How long will you live with life-limiting conditions that may or may not be OK with you?[198]

If we've reached this point in our diagnosis and treatment, the likelihood is that if we're in the hospital, we'll probably die in the hospital. However, while medical technology can keep our vital organs functioning for a long time even after consciousness is lost, it is unreasonable to ask ourselves, "Is this really living?"

THIS IS NEW AND HOW DO WE RESPOND?

Semi- or un-conscious and dependent on life-sustaining equipment to breathe and be fed, one can ask...

1. Is that life?
2. Is it a placeholder for what life might be?
3. Is it a modern life?
4. Is it a medicalized life?
5. Who do we know certainly would be dead if medical advancements were withdrawn?
6. Can someone living in the US today, with all its medical advancements, have confidence that they can experience death on their own terms?
7. Can modern medicine predict the result of a treatment?
8. Can we assume that more treatments, drugs, trials, surgeries, etc. are better?

Usually the answer to questions six, seven and eight are no.

THE PATIENT SELF-DETERMINATION ACT

As a result of the Nancy Cruzan case—the thirty-three-year old woman who ended up in a vegetative state following a car accident and the ensuing legal battle fought by her parents to let her die[199]—the US Congress passed The Patient Self-Determination Act (PSDA) on November 5, 1990. The law is built on the idea of informed consent, a concept popularized by the Nuremberg Code that was established in 1948.[200, 201]

The Patient Self-Determination Act requires that most healthcare institutions (but not individual doctors) that receive federal reimbursements (e.g., Medicare and Medicaid) for services do the following:

1. Give you at the time of admission a written summary of:
   - Your healthcare decision-making rights (each state has developed such a summary for hospitals, nursing homes, and home health agencies to use.)

- The facility's policies with respect to recognizing advance directives.

2. Ask you if you have an advance directive, and document that fact in your medical record if you do. (It is up to you to make sure they get a copy of it).

3. Educate their staff and community about advance directives.

4. Never discriminate against patients based on whether or not they have an advance directive. Thus, it is against the law for them to require either that you have or not have an advance directive.[202]

But beyond the form, The Act does not require attending physicians to ask if the patient has told his/her loved ones their wishes or defined what is an acceptable or unacceptable quality of life.

We all hope we don't face an end like Nancy Cruzan and the PSDA gives us the opportunity and a responsibility to speak up for ourselves while we are able, and before we are faced with a life and death decision. It is also designed to encourage a partnership with our doctors and help facilitate important and necessary patient-physician discussions. Dr. Elizabeth Chaitin writes, "The decision-making power previously relegated to the physician was now to be shared with the ill patient and those chosen as surrogate decision-makers."[203]

Dr. Joan Harrold says, "Today most physicians tend to be collaborative. We want to help a patient navigate the steps they will need to go through and all of that time we want to negotiate and listen to patients, not dictate to them. By offering choices and listening we think it keeps minds open. If we are too definitive we might close the door. I am searching in my discussion to learn the goals of the patient. When I know the patient's goal, not my goal for the patient, I can provide the path to their goal."[204]

This process sounds good, but all of this negotiating can mean the treatment plan gets tossed from physicians, to patients, to families of patients, to nurses, to social workers, to chaplains, to bioethics committees, to courtrooms and to the federal government. Resolving issues requires negotiation between the doctor and an informed assertive patient, which most of us are not. Or maybe we are informed, but we have family members who don't participate with us from the beginning and then panic and try to talk us in or out of our next step.

While the PDSA was designed with good intentions, the law is not working very well. Robin Rome, a palliative nurse practitioner at a Louisiana hospital, says the law was a result of things happening to people that they did not necessarily want. "To comply with this law, every institution has to have something in place asking each patient who gets admitted if they have an advance directive, and this simply becomes an item on a check list. In real life it goes something like this:

	Y	N
Do you have an advanced directive?	☐	☐
	Y	N
Would you like to receive more information on advanced directives?	☐	☐

If the patient answers 'yes' to the first question, then a copy is placed in the chart. If the patient answers 'no' but wants more information, a social worker is notified to meet with the patient for further discussion. If they answer no to both then the subject is dropped."

Rome goes on to say that these questions are asked typically in the admitting department by staff members who are not trained to explore possibilities with patients and only circle the answer provided. These questions are also part of the nursing admission assessment, and while nurses certainly have more advanced training than the staff in admissions, obtaining this information takes time and skill and is among the hundreds of other things nurses have to do when they admit a patient. However, patients often confide in their nurses and tell them things they are afraid to tell the physicians, or patients may practice how to tell the team they want to stop treatment.

Dr. Chaitin says that this law is a "two-dimensional solution to a three-dimensional problem. We have turned to the law to solve a moral problem and it isn't working." She adds that if she could, she would give every person facing a serious diagnosis a "tour guide to their own illness."[205]

THE BUCK STOPS HERE

While health professionals like Robin Rome are working hard to comply with the law, the people whom the law was written to protect—you and me—seem to be working hard to ignore it. In 2012, over twenty years after the law was put in place, less than 25% of American adults have put their expectations for their end-of-life care in writing.[206] Even some of those being admitted to acute care hospitals answer "no" when asked if they have a directive.

Americans have little interest in talking about the possibility of death, and the healthy ones do not understand that the odds they will be able to speak for themselves as they age or become seriously ill are very low. Palliative nurse and instructor Pam Malloy says, "Even nurses who work in hospitals don't have a directive. We live in a death-denying society. At each of our courses—talking about care of the dying, I always ask students how many have an advanced directive. I am always shocked at how many of these professional people, who see death and dying every day do not have an advanced directive."[207]

Both Dr. Joan Harrold and Dr. Barron Lerner told me that the Patient Self-Determination Act is not something they have to think about every day because it is part of them. It is built into the way they practice medicine. They are not intentionally giving patients choices to confuse them; rather they are offering choices because in most cases there are choices to be made. They know the law and respect the law and at the same time they respect their patient's right to choose.[208]

Even the most communicative physicians can leave us confused if we haven't done our homework, if we're in shock or denial about what we've been told, if we are hearing terms we have never heard before, or if we are thinking about what we'll tell our family at the same time the doctor is talking to us.[209] Modern medicine is overwhelming with choices. And the public has expectations that there is a remedy for everything. Health providers try to describe what is in each pill, patch, treatment, transplant, infusion, experiment and procedure. Then they invite you to choose for yourself what you want.

Author and professor at the University of California, San Francisco, Sharon Kaufman writes, "...the choices that must be made are inconceivable. For health professionals, choosing for or against this life-prolonging procedure or that one, choosing death now or death later, is the normal, routine way to move things along. For families and patients it is glaringly clear that these choices are simply impossible. Yet most accept that they or the hospital staff will make choices, and they muddle through them as best they can. Because staff want families to decide and families see choices as impossible, waiting also becomes partly a choice."[210] It is obvious to the healthcare providers that, "Families have no schooling for the situation they are thrown into when someone they love is seriously ill."[211]

Oncologist and palliative medicine physician, Dr. Eric Roeland, and his colleagues write, "Autonomy is the current gold standard approach to patient communication and has grown to the point that patient preference dictates care, even when their choices are not possible or are medically non beneficial."[212]

Giving choice—personal autonomy—to every patient might work if every patient wants it, accepts the responsibility of it, and is willing to become healthcare literate in order to participate in discussions in a meaningful way.[213] Carl Schneider, professor of Law and Internal Medicine at the University of Michigan says, "...while patients largely wish to be informed about their medical circumstances, a substantial number of them do not want to make their own medical decisions or perhaps even participate in those decisions in any very significant way." Professor Schneider goes on to point out that younger people are more likely to want to be involved in making medical decisions than are the elderly, and the sicker a person is, the less likely they are to want to be involved.[214] We can learn from this that when we are weak from an illness and maybe facing end-of-life care choices, we will not be too interested in autonomy.

This autonomy can result in experiences a patient could never anticipate due to the chasing of futile care.[215] Grasping the concept that modern medicine is not in charge of your life even though you might want it to be is vital, and understanding this sooner than later is critical. The Supreme Court told us in black and white that we have the right to die by refusing medical treatment. The court said, "The

Constitution protects the refusal of life-sustaining treatment by competent patients."[216] Then the PSDA spins it into the fact that we have the right to direct our care and we are advised to name a person who can speak for us when we can no longer speak for ourselves.

BAD DECISIONS LEAD TO BAD OUTCOMES

In real life terms, we have the right to refuse the "6,600 potentially dangerous drugs"[217] healthcare providers can prescribe. We can refuse surgery, infusions, implants, transfusions and every other medical care possibility we know about now and all of those that will come to be while we're still breathing. We have the right to refuse water and food. And, there is no law that says you have to dial 911 or let another person do that for you. Right this minute there are plenty of things to refuse, but the list is going to grow as medicine grows its capabilities. We can end up enduring many months or even years with life-prolonging measures or experimental treatment, then on our deathbed say, "I didn't know what I didn't want."

When and if the time comes that the patient cannot speak any longer, the law requires healthcare professionals to consult with the patient's proxy who is chosen by default if the patient has not named one. State laws vary, but in general, proxies are family members.[218] Most of these family members, made proxies by default, have not received any instructions from the patient, and unfortunately for the patient, as Dr. Michael Mitchell says, "When someone is dying there is no such thing as a functional family."[219]

As I write, a friend of mine is saying to everyone who walks into his ICU room, "Please let me die." His wife is his stated healthcare proxy but the law says the proxy doesn't get to start making decisions until the patient loses decisional capacity. Providers are not listening to the patient who is still thinking for himself because the wife overpowers the man in the bed. Even when a patient still has decisional capacity, he can be weakened from a year of treatments and be overwhelmed by a strong family. This happened to my friend. Even though he is a highly educated, accomplished person, who is thinking and talking, his wife's presence in the room and loud demands get the attention of the healthcare providers and my friend's clearly expressed wishes are ignored. This is what I would call a terrible, unintended consequence of the PSDA. My friend is crying out, "I didn't know what I didn't want." He did say he did not want tubes, which he has, but the tubes came from the damage due to the treatments he was not able to stop. The physicians have stated my friend won't recover and there is nothing more they can do and they say he has to go to a nursing home. That is code for: he is stabilized, no longer acute, has to leave the hospital, this is it for this person. Just like when my mom's doctor told me, "This is it. She won't get better. We'll be sending her to a nursing home."

The problem with not naming a proxy and telling that proxy end-of-life wishes happens to famous people, too. Former Israeli Prime Minister Ariel Sharon went into a coma due to a stroke and a brain hemorrhage on January 4, 2006. David Blair, writing for *The Telegraph* reports, "His collapse was so sudden and complete that the doctors at Hadassah University Hospital in Jerusalem advised his family that he should be allowed to die. Yet advanced medical care allowed him to live for another eight years—at least in the physical sense—and receive daily visits from his two sons, Gilad and Omri....His son, Gilad, later summarized the medical advice as: 'Based on the CT scan, the game was over'. However the two brothers insisted that their father must be kept alive."[220] The Prime Minister's stable condition was achieved with a feeding tube and physiotherapy to prevent pressure sores, blood clots and pneumonia which are a constant threat to comatose patients.[221, 222, 223] He finally succumbed on January 11, 2014.[224]

Dr. Jeanne Fitzpatrick and her lawyer sister, Eileen M. Fitzpatrick write, "Only you can choose your end-of-life care. The Cruzan case establishes the important rule that only you can make the decision to discontinue your life support. No one can choose for you (except your named proxy). Moreover, you must clearly and convincingly tell your friends and family what your wishes are—or, better yet, put them in writing."[225]

YOUR PROXY IS YOUR LIFELINE

Doctors who have helped me with this book have taught me that the best hope for the handling of my end-of-life care is a well-chosen, thoughtful surrogate or proxy. In my very first interview with Dr. Jack McNulty, he went to his files and pulled out his healthcare directive for me to see. It's a boiler plate document and at that time he said nothing matters in this except the name of my proxy. Dr. McNulty said in a lecture presented to palliative care nurses, "The living will is not useful because it cannot possibly cover all the conditions I could find myself in when I become seriously ill. The person named as surrogate or proxy in the advance directive is the key to my attending physicians knowing what to do with me as an illness progresses."

My efforts to get my own death right kept me asking questions. Dr. McNulty sent me to Dr. Jean Kutner, former president of the American Academy of Hospice and Palliative Care Medicine, who told me, "A living will is often not very useful. I took the advance directive my attorney provided and simplified it. I removed much of the specifics found in the living will section because what matters is the person I have named to speak for me."[226]

Dr. Lerner agrees that the person you name to speak for you is the key to the end-of-life decision-making process. He is one of the doctors who granted me an extended interview for this book and he also read this entire chapter to make sure I don't give any bad or wrong information. As part of my surveying of how doctors want to die and because of his writing about his father's medical practice, then his father's death, I asked him to offer some specific advice for how to choose a proxy. His proxy is his wife, yet she is a judge and an attorney. He also advises you put it in writing and tell your proxy straight, "If I change my mind at the end, do not listen to me."

If you have a look at my directive you will see that I added his instruction. You will also see that my directive is not about treatments; it is about how I want to live out my days. You will also see that I did not name my husband as my proxy. First, he is three years older than me and just looking at data I can assume that he will predecease me. Even more important to me is that my husband does not have to deal with providers, he can just hold my hand. I learned from watching my father. Everyone agreed he was tough; some would even say hard-hearted, yet I watched this very strong man shrink in the face of my mother's terrible stroke. He didn't ask doctors or nurses questions and appeared to me to be in a haze of sadness. Why should my husband have to pull himself up and sort things out with doctors when he might just want to be a sweet presence for me?

"Get yourself a fighter to be your proxy. And name a back-up, too. The end of any life is complicated and will require courage and clear thinking. This is partly because we seem to conflate trying harder with better outcomes and so often the trying does not lead to meaningful recovery." – Dr. Barron Lerner

Dr. Carolyn McClanahan said, "Some adult children can be excellent surrogates for their parents but some don't have the personality characteristics it takes. Choose a thoughtful person who has taken time to listen to you now and knows you and one who is strong enough to resist pushback from other family members. As an ER doctor I don't believe it is my fellow physicians or all of the teams that work with us who are pushing for patients to be kept alive. Often we do what we know how to do under pressure of trying to please loved ones."[227]

Dr. Elizabeth Chaitin says, "If you choose a child as your proxy, avoid the quiet one. Choose the obnoxious one, the one who will not take 'no' for an answer. Just make sure that child knows what you want and that he or she can work to get you what you want, and not what they want. If you don't have children or you don't want your children to have to speak for you, choose a minister or a neighbor or the child of a dear friend or a niece or nephew."[228]

Another healthcare provider told me that he is not sure that his named proxy, his wife, would follow his end-of-life instructions so he added his own backup. He writes, "I authorize my physician, Dr. Jones, to override my wife if she fails or refuses to follow my advance directive as it is written. I would ask that my doctor then work with my family to come to some solution that would meet with my wishes as outlined within my advance directive."

The job of the surrogate is huge.[229] "In nearly 80% of the 2.5 million deaths occurring in US hospitals each year, proxies make 70% to 90% of intensive care unit decisions to withhold or withdraw life-sustaining treatment. Therefore, proxies' decisions likely influence nearly 1.5 million deaths per year."[230]

The proxies doing the 70% to 90% of the decision making are not proxies chosen by the patient. They are the defaults. Most proxies receive their power as the unintended consequence of a law that gives power to the uninformed. Think back to my mom's story. Doctors were doing their best. Then Mom ended up in a kind of vegetative state with no hope that she would come back even close to where she was before hospitalization. I had to intervene, but in most situations no one is informed by the patient in regards to what they want.

Choosing a proxy (instead of settling for a "default") and talking with that person is not too hard to do, and it is all made legal with one piece of paper. Physicians are used to speaking with proxies, and the proxy can deal with current patient conditions and information rather than depend upon what could be imagined and written about in a living will. Basically, "Durable powers of attorney [(proxies)] are—as these things go—simple, direct, modest, straightforward, and thrifty."[231]

There are obstacles to choosing a person to speak for us on a future date that is impossible for us to mark on a calendar. It would be great if we could call a friend and say, "Hey, I am going to get very sick in 2017 and in November of that year I will need you to talk with my doctors. Could you be available to do that for me?"

OBSTACLES TO NAMING A PROXY[232]

The proxy you name is probably not a medical professional, and so that person you name will be learning on the fly while caring for you, a seriously ill loved one.

Physician-related
- Discomfort with the topic
- Lack of institutional support
- Lack of reimbursement for time spent in a discussion about this topic
- Lack of time
- Waiting for the patient to initiate the discussion

Nurse-related
- Discomfort with topic
- Lack of time
- Various rules on whether nurses can witness such forms
- When nurse tells team the patient is ready, team may say it is too early to ask for a proxy

Patient-related
- Fear of burdening family or friends
- Health literacy
- Lack of interest or knowledge: "I don't want to think about it"
- Social isolation, lack of reliable proxy
- Spiritual and cultural traditions
- Waiting for the physician to initiate the discussion

Once you do name a proxy, physicians happily engage with that person so that you receive the end-of-life care you want. While time-consuming, emotionally-challenging and filled with uncertainty, there is no escaping these difficult situations.[233]

CHOOSE A PROXY NOT A COMMITTEE

If we jointly give spouse and adult children the authority to direct physicians as conditions change and care unfolds in unpredictable ways, we have created a potential powder keg and have thrown the doctors into a most terrible situation. They are physicians not psychotherapists. If our extended family can't decide where to gather for a holiday, do you really think as a group they can decide what should happen to us in a life and death situation? Think of the famous adage, "A camel is a horse designed by a committee."

And, even when your spouse and children can finally come to a conclusion, will one person be blamed for killing you? Or will one person be blamed for getting you what some social workers call "the trifecta of elder care"—a trachea (short for tracheostomy), a PEG (feeding tube from the outside of the body to the stomach) and a slot in a nursing home?

Over and over I have read about family members who are not able to set their emotions aside and let their parent or child have a gentle death. One palliative care nurse told me, "Children are in denial about their parents' mortality," so this is a good reason not to name a child as your healthcare proxy. And often a well-thought-out advance directive is overridden by adult children or other family members. This is usually because there are unresolved issues. Some family member feels guilty that they mistreated you or never came to visit you before and after you became ill. One palliative care physician used the euphemism "the guilty daughter from California," to describe these situations. That person wants to keep you alive so they can reconcile with you, make it up to you, somehow cram in the love that they didn't have time to give in the past. They may demand that the hospital and its staff keep you alive—while the medical reality is that you are not going to recover, let alone come back close to the person they used to know. In the case of veterans, some families may want them to live as long as possible so they (the family) can receive certain benefits.[234] And it is possible that some of the most well-intentioned parents may be keeping their sick children alive past the point of recovery so they can assuage any possible future guilt.

While interviewing the director of a hospice, I saw a very sad man pacing the hallways. The director teared up and said, "His wife is dying and he is being emotionally abused by her siblings. The wife was at MD Anderson Cancer Center, and after months of trying, the physicians told the husband that there was nothing more they could do for his wife and together the decision was made to put her into hospice care. Now the wife's siblings, from far-flung parts of the United States, are calling him and telling him that he is killing their sister."

Unresolved issues manifest in many ways. A man I will call Martin (not his real name), was a high-powered attorney who at the age of fifty-eight was diagnosed with lung cancer that had already spread to his brain. The medical team who made the diagnoses knew Martin well, because he had handled legal work for some of them. They were in tears when they told him that they would recommend no cancer treatment and they would start a morphine drip right away. Martin's wife jumped in and said, "That is not at all what we need to do. He can and must fight this. We have three children in preschool."

Months later, the wife watched her husband die slowly and confessed to family gathered at the home, "I am enjoying this. I want the bastard to suffer. He is getting what he deserves. He's cheated on me over and over again though there was no way I was going to divorce him and give up this lifestyle. Well, the joke is on him. Now who's humiliated? He always tried to control everyone and everything now he can't even control his bladder." Martin was in diapers, living in a care facility. Thanks to his lucrative professional career, he was receiving disability insurance payments of $20,000 a month—a healthy income by most standards except that the family expenses were running $35,000 a month. Martin's care alone for the past twelve months had cost $60,000 out of pocket. His ownership in the law firm was sold to Martin's partners, but family debts continued to pile up as they burned through savings. While the wife looks from the outside like the loving caretaker, the family goes bankrupt as she extracts the revenge she was impotent to wield while her husband was healthy and vital.

This, of course, is not the only case of a caregiver who is sicker than the patient. I also heard a story from a palliative care nurse about a son in prison who fought with and overruled his eleven siblings in the argument to keep their mother alive though she was in a vegetative state. One psychologist suggests that the son feels guilty that he has dishonored his mother and wants to get to her bedside and tell her that he is the good son who is fighting for her life.

My friends who are moms tell me that their children, just like the son in prison, are going to kick and scream to keep them alive. Then they add, "But they know I do not want to be kept alive by machines." Dr. Kutner said, "When I ask my older patients if their children know what kind of care they want they always say, 'Oh yes.' Then I go to the adult children and the adult children have no idea."[235] More than one social worker has told me that they have worked with hundreds of families who have never heard the dying person say a word about how they want the end of their life to unfold.

Each of these stories shows that death can be as traumatic for the living as for those who are actually dying. Caregivers' and family members' reactions—good and bad—are shaped by many things, including experiences with the dying person, religious beliefs, cultural norms and last but not least, unresolved issues.

Not choosing a proxy means your case defaults to next of kin or, in some states, parties of interest. And the next of kin and parties of interest can get into some ugly disagreements. And, if you are famous, these arguments will end up in the press.[236]

"In palliative medicine, we recognize that serious illness involves uncertainty and that facing uncertainty is hard and sometimes produces anxiety for patients, families, and clinicians. We strive to address this uncertainty so people can plan and adjust goals to have a greater sense of well-being." - DR. LAURA MORRISON[238]

PERHAPS THE PENDULUM IS SWINGING

While the PSDA is not without its faults, patients are fortunate that thousands of physicians, nurses, social workers and chaplains have been working with the PSDA for decades. These interdisciplinary palliative care services teams see the flaws in the law and yet they embrace the difficult conversations. They are trained to tell people they are dying. Social workers and chaplains on the care teams work hard to understand the emotional, psychological, social and cultural side of the patient and their family. Moreover, research shows patients and families are more satisfied when they have received interdisciplinary palliative care services.[237]

Hospice and Palliative Medicine became an official subspecialty listed with the American Board of Medical Specialities in 2006 and according to the Center to Advance Palliative Care, in 2012 there were more than 1,700 hospital-based palliative care programs.[239] This number is growing each year and in the hands of this new specialty, the patient who doesn't want to or is unsure how to make any decisions will find courageous professionals who listen and advise. Palliative care is also where the patient can find the truth about disease trajectory, treatment side effects, how aging affects outcomes, advanced pain and symptom management and help beyond medicine to cope with stress and emotional pain.[240]

Dr. Eric Roeland says, "As disease advances and prognosis worsens, the patient loses autonomy and viable treatment options become fewer...the clinician plays a larger role in decision making, not by taking control but rather by identifying viable medical options."[241]

You want the palliative team knowing about you as there will be a time when your doctor will say, "This is all I can do for you. We've tried everything." Your disease pressed beyond your doctor's area of specialty. However, the palliative team is trained to provide symptom and pain management plus help with grief/loss/bereavement and with spiritual angst. When a doctor says, "There's nothing more I can do," it does not mean there's nothing more medicine can do. Request that a person who works in palliative care be brought in to speak with you and your family.

Progress is being made to deal with the debilitating end-of-life dilemma that modern medicine has created. However, the inch-by-inch progress can be sped up when each of us take our own debilitating end-of-life dilemma personally. We can simply use the existing law to state clearly how we want to leave this earth. With one sheet of paper we can do an end-run around the formidable, institutionalized standards of care. We may use the existing system then choose to change our focus. It's our choice and we need an advocate as a backup.

Our goal should be a circle of care that includes family, friends, social workers, nurses and physicians. This circle should create a world where patients trust their providers, medicine doesn't fear lawyers, doctors do their very best for every patient, patients and their families have some personal financial incentives to stop demanding futile care, and modern medicine is quick to admit that death is natural.

ELIMINATE THE BURDEN

I do not want to be a burden or a bother or a worry, now or in the future. To put the puzzle pieces in place so I am none of these things, I have chosen my proxy, also known as the durable power of attorney. She is a distant niece whom I chose because she is a nurse with a backbone of steel. She is thirty-four years my junior, she has listened to my wishes, she has read my healthcare directive (which you can find on pages 135-137) and can be trusted not to fold under the pressure of modern medical institutions. Physicians don't intimidate her, and other family members will back off when she enters the room. If for some reason she is not available, my backup is my neighbor Dr. Pat Gary, an ER and internal medicine doctor whom you read about in Chapter 1. From the support she has provided as I gathered this information, I know she believes as strongly in avoiding a medicalized death as I do.

It is important to know that while it may appear I chose these women because they are healthcare professionals, the truth is that I chose them because they fit the criteria I suggest you use as you make your choice. Two years ago I gave my doctor a physical copy of my directive, which includes my proxy's name. Because the physician is in the out-patient clinic of a hospital, I can also place my directive in the electronic record for him and all to see.

Doctors cannot and do not want to make end-of-life decisions alone.[242] Your doctor might be willing if you are very clear and have a close relationship, but at the end of your life there could be as many as twelve physicians taking care of you. It can get especially complex, so for your sake and out of a sense of responsibility to those you love, it is important to choose for yourself now and ensure the end-of-life care you want.

Naming your proxy is the biggest gift you can give to your entire circle of care, which includes your doctors. This is serious, but it should not be that hard for you to do. It is possible that you have no biological family or you do not want to choose a family member for this task. Or, like me, you may choose a relative you have gained through marriage. Will it hurt the feelings of your daughter if you choose your son's wife? Not if you explain your thinking. Not if you do it now while you are healthy—when there is no emergency, while logic can prevail, while things are hypothetical and probably distant. Your proxy choice is your decision to make as you see fit. You are standing on a Supreme Court decision backed up by a law.

STEP 4 in taking control of end-of-life decisions is providing specific instructions to loved ones and choosing one person who will speak for you when you are no longer able to speak for yourself. You may designate your proxy on page 211. Please answer the questions and fill in the blanks you will find on pages 202-213 of the MY WAY WORKBOOK.

CHAPTER 5

LIVE FULLY ALL THE WAY TO THE END

Y ou know you are going to die. You just don't know what day. You've got the fear of death under your belt. It's conquered and behind you. Let's go after the other fears that cripple, deplete, tear down and run roughshod over your *kardia*—that is your heart.

My friend who is eighty-five had a quadruple bypass at the age of eighty-three and is now in the care of a cardiologist who has a five-part treatment: meditation, yoga, exercise, diet and medication. Note the order. What do parts one, two and three treat? Homeostasis, or the soup his heart is swimming in. While doctors are good at telling you that you feel bad because you have a blocked artery, which means you don't have enough oxygen reaching heart tissue, they are not so good at telling you how the artery got blocked. Doctors treat the heart as a pump of oxygen-rich blood. You are in charge of creating the environment in which the life-sustaining pump operates.

MOVING FROM DENIAL TO ACCEPTANCE

In his book, *The Book of Awakening: Having the Life You Want by Being Present to the Life You Have,* Mark Nepo shares questions that can help us accept the inevitability of our death and remove the fear. Take some time to answer them now.

What is your greatest fear about dying?

What is your greatest fear about living?

Do these fears have anything in common?

How would you shape your life if you didn't have these fears?

What if you shaped your life in this way anyway?

MORE THAN A MUSCLE

The word cardiology comes from the Greek word, *kardia.* It can mean the seat of the soul, the emotions—the feelings that sweep over and occupy the mind. Philosophers say kardia means the inner life, intuition, inner self, will, the source of desire, decision-making and passion. When a high-jump coach tells athletes to throw their hearts over the bar, the coach is not talking about the pump in the middle of the chest.

For good or bad, our kardia, the seat of our soul, moves the mind. When your logic based upon analysis says one thing and your heart says another, you go with your heart, right? Or, you go with your logic then beat yourself up for years for not going with your heart. Or, you go with your logic and do not work on eliminating the heart-disconnect so you live in heart-head conflict. This tension is stress, and chronic stress, "increases your risk of getting diseases that make you sick, or if you have such a disease, stress increases the risk of your defenses being overwhelmed by disease."[243]

AS GOES THE HEART

It is not enough to plan for a peaceful death, we have to live into it. We've already learned that the person who lives well, dies well, but what does that mean? We have to live the life that leads us seamlessly to a gentle death; we all have to get a hold of the invisible, now.

Somewhere between 1985 and 1992, in one of the many sermons I heard my pastor, Cecil Sherman, deliver, he said something I will never forget. I have passed it along to many friends when they were hurting. He said, no matter what things look like from the outside, "Life is fair. It breaks everybody's heart." In 2010, Dr. Sherman died at the age of eighty-two of complications from a heart attack.

Except for all the killings in wars, the number one killer of human beings throughout the history of civilization is the heart stopping. Your heart will stop one day and between now and then you have millions of tiny decisions to make that will give you vitality all the way to the last beat or will turn you into a deeply nuanced web of entanglements.

David, the Jewish shepherd who became Israel's king, wrote the prayer, "Create in me a clean heart"[244] after he had been caught murdering the husband of the woman he wanted for himself. King David knew he was in heart trouble, and he was not thinking about his cholesterol. He was aching so deeply, he had to pour out the ache to his God. He had to get this ache off his chest and out of his kardia.

In contrast with King David, who chose to get his heart right, Cornelius Gurlitt (1933-2014), never murdered anyone but also did not appear concerned with "heart issues" until the final years of his life. He was a hoarder of art inherited from his father, Hildebrand Gurlitt (1895-1956). The collection was worth a billion dollars,[245] and Cornelius said it was the only thing in life he ever loved. Hildebrand was an art dealer and took orders from Hilter. He was told to sell modern art that came to him in mysterious ways (*Vanity Fair* reports he actually did some of the stealing with his own bare hands[246]), as the money was needed by the Nazis.[247]

In the process of obeying orders, it seems as if Hildebrand Gurlitt kept plenty for himself. His son grew up with works by Chagall, Beckman, Matisse and more. When authorities entered Cornelius' 1,000 square foot apartment in 2012 and removed 1,280 paintings and prints[248]—the loves of his life—he was in shock. These pieces were his, since his father had died in 1956, and the boy had never left home. He lived with his mother and the stolen art until she died in 1968, then he had it all to himself. It was all his.

In 2012, authorities confiscated the remaining art collection and two years later he was found dead in his apartment. Upon his death, *The Wall Street Journal* reported, "Mr. Gurlitt had spent most of the two years since the raid brooding over his lost treasure."[249] We can only speculate that Mr. Gurlitt's last days were filled with torment knowing that the art he loved so much had been stolen by his father, all ill-gotten gain that could only negate his long-held belief that he was the son of a hero. King David realized he was a fraud and worked to clear his soul with his God. In contrast, Cornelius embedded his self-deception, guilt, shame and lies in his heart and apparently took them all to the grave.

Clearly our life choices impact our hearts. We hide our secrets, go along to get along, accommodate, obfuscate, stuff down, tolerate or pretend, but at great risk because our body experiences the poison of such behavior, and it seeps into every crevice, corner, cell and molecule like an IV drip of toxic waste. Fear, anger, bitterness, regret, remorse, pride, self-indulgence—drip, drip, drip. Or like King David, we can look at our truth and make things right within ourselves and between the important people in our lives and our maker, and the healing of the kardia makes our end more peaceful.

LETTING GO IS POWERFUL MEDICINE

As you contemplate your wishes for the end of your life, look also at what you may be holding onto in this life right now that needs to be let go—anger, bitterness, regrets, fear of being exposed, fear of being alone, fear of nothing to do if you retire, fear your children won't come see you, fear your daughter-in-law won't let you see your grandchildren, fear you'll live longer than your money lasts, fear of boredom, fear of looking back over what you may decide has been a wasted life.

Fear creates enemies. Any "enemies" you have in your life are there because you are afraid of them. The all-powerful king of Israel, Saul, was afraid of a young man named David.[250] This fear brought on depression, paranoia, and manipulative schemes to get the young David killed; eventually the fear was so great in Saul that he himself tried to murder David.

Shakespeare's King Lear was afraid of retirement. He tried to give up responsibility and hold onto power. He had one lovely daughter and two terrible ones. His paranoia turned into anger and he ran the lovely one off to marry the King of France. Next he bounced from one terrible daughter to the other dragging along with him his madness and one hundred knights.

King Lear's physician today would diagnose him with dementia, for sure. More detrimental than dementia, though, was his desperate need to hold on to enemies and power. Lear's eventual fate is an excellent example of the adage, "Your sins will find you out."[251] If you are not part of a religious tradition that believes in good and evil, you can translate this to mean that karma will turn around and bite you. While you may delegate your heart, the pump, to your cardiologist, you have to take personal responsibility for your kardia as it is way beyond the competencies of physicians.

When King Lear discovered that Cordelia, his devoted daughter, had been slaughtered, he died of a broken heart—which doctors today call "stress-introduced cardiomyopathy." King Lear was lucky because had Shakespeare been writing today, he would have had someone call 911. Lear would have been resuscitated in the ambulance and brought into the ER where as many as six or seven healthcare professionals would have gone to work to stabilize his heart. Then he would have been released from the ER or ICU to carry on with his tortured soul, demented brain and without the darling of his life.

BUILD YOURSELF A BAGGAGE-FREE FUTURE

What baggage do we want with us in our deathbed? The good news is that no one needs to have any unnecessary baggage today or tomorrow. One of my generation's songwriters, Kenny Loggins, gave us the song of decompression. You probably know it, "Loose, footloose, kick off your Sunday shoes." I can imagine you can sing the whole chorus to yourself right now.

We have to voluntarily let go of certain aspects of our existence in this world and, at the same time, adjust to what gets taken from us without our approval. This is tricky, because losing a friend to a disease might shake our confidence and send us back to old fearful thoughts of dying. Even if you have accepted your eventual death and it holds no fear for you, you might start thinking, "My friend is dead. I'm scared I'm next."

We have lots of loss ahead of us. We have spent a life acquiring, and as we move forward, much of life will be about letting go and losing. We will lose hair, a business card with a title on it, strength in our muscles, being in demand, thrill of adventure, friends, party invitations, our love of running up the stairs. When we start looking for how to live on one floor of our two-story houses, we just lost our entire second floor. It's there but we can't or don't want to go there, it's just hanging over our heads.

How do we learn to balance what we must lose with what we are able to keep? I have a good example living under my own roof. Bruce, my husband, was born in 1947, and he still thinks he is thirty. While in the yard one day, he threw a bamboo stalk at a bird that had been stalking us. With the desire to please me—he had been yelling at, whistling at (with a ref's high pitch whistle meant to stop the action on the basketball court) and in general grousing at the annoying bird—Bruce gave all his effort, and threw out his arm. It turned into huge pain he did not understand. He's been a strong physical man all his life and this pain was new to him. So, like we all do, he went first to his primary care physician (PCP) who gave him a pain killer and said nothing was torn or broken. The PCP sent him to a physical therapist which turned out to be just too simple, meaning Bruce learned the exercises and did them on his own and he didn't need to go back. Still, the pain continued and the PCP sent him to the orthopedist who said nothing was torn or broken and gave him a stronger pain killer. We decided if his arm goes out again, he will just take Advil® and forgo the appointments and the expense because it was time that healed the hurt.

Bruce understands life because he has struggled with the hard things all of his life. He has built a brain muscle that can find answers and solve problems. We all hope to have this kind of vitality after we pass sixty and seventy years of life on this earth. Bruce's kardia is loose, footloose. He is baggage-free and flying forward. He simply has to pay respect to the old body that carries around his still-young mind. Our muscles grow from birth until we turn thirty, then we can lose 3% to 5% of our muscle mass every decade. But, there is hope. Dr. John E. Morley says, "Protein together with resistance exercise stops the loss of muscle that is associated with aging."

THE FABULOUS JOHN E. MORLEY

I offer my encounter with John E. Morley as another example. He is a physician, geriatrician, endocrinologist, professor of medicine and writer. He is the author of twenty-one books and 1,000 research and educational articles in addition to many short pieces published regularly in the *St. Louis Dispatch*. One of these 1,000 articles, "Top Ten Topics in Aging,"[252] was assigned in a graduate course I was taking. I learned so much when I read it that I decided Dr. Morley might be the right physician to advise me as I gathered the information here. When we spoke on the phone, my first question was, "Would you be willing to advise me on the book I am writing about how we can all get ourselves a good death?"

Before I could blink he said, "No, no. I'm not interested in death at all and simply I'm not up on it. However, I will say that dying should be fun."[253]

I laughed then, and he kept me laughing during the entire conversation. I couldn't get him to talk about dying, except he did tell me what he is going to do if he gets a serious diagnosis and how he plans to spend his final days. I asked him to share advice about what we all need to do to live fully all the way to the end.

1. Stop taking so many drugs. Too many of my patients come to me from other physicians all loaded down with drugs. I think some physicians want to kill their patients. Most drugs you need you should be able to purchase for $4 a month at Walmart.
2. If you are over sixty-five eat anything you want, and I would like you to eat fish two to four times a week.
3. Speaking of alcohol, one drink per day for a woman and two for a man.
4. If you are over seventy, try to find a geriatrician, although there are only 7,000 of us to go around.
5. If you don't spend twelve minutes per day doing a bit of aerobic, a bit of resistance and a bit of balancing exercises you might as well shoot yourself.

Well, at that I had to stop him because I know how to do aerobic and resistance but I had no clue what he meant by balancing exercise. So he taught me right there on the spot. He said stand up, face forward, now stand on one leg and close your eyes. You should be able to do that on each leg for ten to fifteen seconds. At first I could only do five seconds. Now I can do over fifteen seconds, so I do not have to go out and shoot myself.

From a few of his *St. Louis Dispatch* articles I learned these additional things.

1. Telomeres are the caps at the end of each chromosome that protect it from damage. Olive oil, fish, fruits, vegetables, some quiet meditation time and perhaps a daily glass of wine increases telomere length, which is a marker for longevity.
2. Walking eleven minutes a day can help you live nearly two years longer.
3. Walking thirty minutes twice a week slows brain shrinkage.
4. If you retire, loneliness is a risk. So stay connected, perhaps by volunteering.
5. Being sick makes you old. Being sick drains your energy. The age at which you are dealing with sickness matters, so as you age, don't get sick. Avoid sick people and don't think about being sick.

THE HARDEST PART IS NOT PHYSICAL

Everyone can do what Dr. Morley tells us to do. It is so simple. You don't have to join a gym, or hire a trainer or get special clothes or shoes. You don't even have to buy weights. We can manage the physical fitness. But can we manage the emotional fitness?

Ira Byock is a prominent thought leader in the end-of-life community. In interviews, palliative and hospice nurses all seem to quote Dr. Byock. He is a physician who has spent his entire career in hospice and palliative care and currently serves as chief medical officer of the Providence Institute for Human Caring. I have spoken to some of these practitioners who explain to me that modern medicine can mitigate all physical pain in the dying process, but medicine can't mitigate emotional pain, and suffering in death will happen for the person who is not emotionally well. Caregivers say that the patient who has lived well will die well—and they are not talking about physical fitness.

Dr. Byock was given the lifetime achievement award from the American Academy of Hospice and Palliative Medicine in 2014. Additionally, he has been recognized by many other prestigious groups during the past three decades and has written three important books: *Dying Well* (1997), *The Four Things That Matter Most* (2004) and *The Best Possible Care* (2012).

What I learned from his three books is how hard the physicians and their teams in palliative care work. He never says he is working hard—he simply writes about patients and families and the human condition as he sees it unfolding in the most sacred of moments.

This is the reason Dr. Byock wrote *The Four Things That Matter Most*. He put his finger on the root of the emotional suffering and encourages us to take care of this before it becomes suffocating deathbed baggage. Such a cause of suffering is called "unfinished business" by Gestalt therapists. The good news is that, "Previously unrecognized emotions relating to an incident in the past can be explored and acknowledged in the present."[254]

BAGGAGE IS PERSONAL

Dr. Byock teaches that much of our unfinished business can be handled without too much difficulty. He says that we must master eleven words if we want to die well. And, by mastering these eleven words, and by using them now, maybe even decades ahead of death, we can be one of the people who enjoy a gentle leaving. Here are the eleven words:

Please forgive me. I forgive you. Thank you. I love you.[255]

Before I knew Dr. Byock, my dad showed me how to say the first three words. When he was dying, he asked me what mistakes he had made with me. I thought a minute and said that there was a boy he did not want me to date because he was Catholic, and I thought that was a mistake. Dad said, "You're right, that was a mistake. Anything else?" I said, "No. You were a great dad." On page 188, you can read more of what my dad said.

One psychologist gave me an exercise for letting go of my anger towards others. This fits with words four, five and six. When someone hurts you deeply, you can let the person go out of your life entirely or you can let go of the specific hurt. I have said words four, five and six many times both literally and figuratively. One way to do this figuratively is with visualization.

Close your eyes. Imagine the person you are letting go sitting in a beautiful comfortable chair inside a crystal clear bubble. The bubble is like a balloon with a huge silk ribbon tied to close it off so that the air will stay inside. You have a pair of shiny silver scissors and you let the ribbon slip through your hands so the bubble balloon is now floating high in a big blue sky. You cut the ribbon and the bubble balloon and the person you are letting go is allowed to float off in all goodness and light. And you say, "I forgive you. I am sure you didn't intend to hurt me. I want only goodness for you." Conversely, if someone comes to you and asks forgiveness, you give it—you must. It is so easy to say words four, five and six.

On page 188 you will find writing assignments. Take this opportunity to write thank you notes and love letters to the people in your life. I've given you examples from a few of mine to demonstrate that you do not have to be Shakespeare to tell another person how you feel in writing.

Dear Bruce,

You, my darling, are my one and only.

What a gift God gave to me when he put you in my life. What fun it is to live with the bravest person I know. What joy it is to live with a man who is seeking after the heart of God. How freeing it is to live with a man who knows no fear. How comforting it is to live with a man who tells me that he loves and adores me. How invigorating to live with a man who never wants to go down the same road twice. What an adventure you are.

When you wrap your arms around me, I feel safe. When you call to me, I feel wanted. When you eat my cooking, I feel appreciated. I can't imagine earth-bound living without you.

I love you with all my heart.

Hattie

Dear darling LG,

You are the amazing truth teller, and I know I need a truth teller in my life! Not only are you brilliant, you're the best storyteller in the whole world, which makes our conversations more fun than going to a movie. Your commitment to honesty means you don't mind kicking me in the rear end when it needs to be kicked. And even though it might hurt, I know I am better for it. Thank you for being my true-blue, glam-queen, truth-telling friend.

Love, love, love,
Hattie

My Dear MG,

Thank you for being the one I run to after Bruce is sick and tired of hearing me complain about whatever little thing isn't going my way. You know my life has never seen hard hardship but you sweetly listen and keep on loving me through it all. One of the most beautiful things you ever did for me and my siblings was to write about your memories of our mother. So many of the people who were at her funeral service never knew her like you knew her. They never got to sit at her dinner table and eat her homemade fried chicken and save room for the chocolate mayonnaise cake. You are always in my heart.

Love,
Hattie

Dear MJ,

It's a bit intimidating to write a thank you note to a writer so as our dear Ashley would say, "Don't judge me." I want you to know what a pure joy you are to me. I want to thank you, deeply and profoundly, for being my friend through thick and thin and with a lot of thin the last ten years. Your voice makes me smile as does the beautiful picture I have of you smack dab in the center of my adored-persons bulletin board. I know if I am ever in trouble that you will come running to me. Thank you for being a solid rock of a person and for letting me be a little part of your life.

Love,
Hattie

THE MISSING LOVE LETTER

My friend Suzanne's father, Joe, had been going downhill for about five years when, at the age of eighty-seven, his blood pressure had shot up so high that 911 was called and he went into the hospital.

It was a Tuesday evening and Suzanne rushed to his side and found her mother, Emily, sitting in a chair next to the bed but not too close. Joe had his eyes closed and his mouth open, constantly talking, but only once in awhile could Suzanne make out what he was saying, which was her name or her mother's name. The nurses were sedating him but he kept talking and his entire body was in an agitated state.

Suzanne kept telling her father to relax and that he was in good hands. Nothing the caregivers did worked, and he did not sleep; he had not one calm moment for four days and nights. The high blood pressure medicine had affected his kidneys and the doctor came in to say that he thought it was time to move Joe to a hospice care facility. Suzanne wanted to take her father home, but the doctor felt Joe needed a bit more support for a gentle passing. The move took place on Friday morning.

Saturday evening Joe was still in an agitated state, and finally Suzanne got the idea that since everyone in the core family was present except for her husband, James, just maybe Joe wanted to talk with James. Suzanne and James live in another state and Suzanne has made so many trips to the bedsides of her parents, it was always hard for James to know if it was time for him to come, too.

Suzanne told her father that James was on the phone and wanted to speak to him. For the first time in five days Joe opened his eyes, relaxed his body and stopped talking. James said, "Dad, you need to know that it is OK for you to leave us. I will take care of Emily. You can depend on me. We will miss you, and at the same time, we will be fine. You can relax as every detail will be attended to by me with help from Suzanne and Robert (Joe and Emily's son)."

Joe then closed his eyes, stayed perfectly relaxed and died eleven hours later.

Think hard: what is important to the person who is dying? What are their values and their ways of doing things? When Joe died, James would be the oldest man in the family. James is ten years older than

Suzanne and Suzanne is eight years older than her brother, Robert. Joe was born in 1927 and his generation tends to be traditional, deferring to the oldest child and often to the oldest boy, skipping over any daughters who might be older. In Joe's formative years, men were expected to take care of things. Joe must have thought it not proper to expect his beautiful daughter to take over his hard work of caring for Emily, even though that is exactly what Suzanne had been doing for both of her parents as they lost functionality over the last five years.

Suzanne told me that her father had told her mother a week before the last hospitalization that he was dying. Her mom said something like, "No you're not." Perhaps Joe interpreted this statement as, "No you can't die, because who will take care of me?"

Suzanne told me that while her mom sat vigil with her, her mom never reached out to Joe, never expressed affection, deferred every decision and took no action. Most likely, she was in shock seeing her husband of more than sixty years leaving her. Or, perhaps she was thinking ahead to the overwhelming task of deciding what she would eat for breakfast on her first day alone in her own home. Or, possibly, Emily was subconsciously angry that Joe was leaving her alone to care for herself when Joe had always fulfilled that role.

I wonder how these final hours might have been different *if* Emily had prepared years ago for this moment. Would she have been able to lovingly whisper in his ear, "It's OK darling. You go on. I'll be fine. Suzanne and James and Robert are here for me. They will make sure I am taken care of. Even though they are not you, you taught them well. You go on. I'll be fine. I'll always love you"? Would Joe have relaxed, rather than having not one restful moment for 120 hours even after heavy sedation? That is the power of human will. Joe desperately needed something and would not rest until he got it.

Or, were Joe and Emily merely products of their generation? The husband was the provider by virtue of his work and income. The wife was in charge of the household—meals, children, laundry, housekeeping, discipline, entertaining and most importantly, taking care of the husband. Even if she was ready to take the reins of her own life and household, it would have been difficult for Emily to go against everything upbringing, society and culture taught her about her role as a wife and mother. Times have changed, and today's relationships are driven by a different set of rules. But when one partner or a significant family member dies, these relationships can become just as confusing, complex and overwhelming as Joe and Emily's if the hard work of planning is not done in advance.

Not only do you have to get ready to die yourself, you have to get ready and be ready to let any person in your life have a peaceful, sweet, calm, and gentle passing on. You have to grow up your inside self. Nature grows you up physically, but growing up inside takes your own initiative. No one can do it for you. Joe was lucky to have Suzanne, James and Robert to make his ending more peaceful—and make this time a gentler transition for his wife as well.

We don't want to be Emily. We want to tell people now that they can leave us and we will be fine. We don't want to be baggage on the deathbed of any other soul. We don't want to be unprepared to live alone. If life has not previously provided us with the chance to mature and realize this, it is important to leave our emotional childhood behind now.

My friend Cindy is one of six children. When her mother was dying, each of her fine, grown up children went individually to her bed and said things like, "I love you, Mom. Thank you for bringing me into the world, and thank you for loving me so much that you were even tough on me. Thank you for teaching me what I needed to know to live in this crazy, complex world. You have done your work. It's OK for you to let go and leave. I'll miss you, and at the same time I'll be fine. You will always be alive right here in my heart," or, "Your DNA is right here pumping in me. You'll be with me here even though I don't get to go with you now."

TRAVELING LIGHT THE REST OF THE WAY

Patterns are comfortable but ruts are deadly. To further ensure that we end our lives with no regrets, we need to get going on the things we want to do.

Deb, a palliative care nurse, was with a patient who was dying. He said the only regret he had was that he had not gone to Paris. Deb, who has a very big job in a big hospital, went home and asked her husband if he could arrange to take off work right away. A few weeks later the two were in Paris, because Deb, too, had always wanted to go to Paris. Her dying patient had taught her how to live her life.

Don't quit. Don't retire; reinvent. Don't sit too much; get out and do. My interpretation of my faith tells me we are to work six days a week and rest on the seventh, and we are to do this until we drop dead. The stress of doing nothing kills. The stress man himself, Hans Selye, said we all have a sweet stress spot.

> Stress is the salt of life; few people would like to live in an existence of no runs, no hits, no errors. Yet it is beneficial for the human machine to rest periodically; hence the development of various religious and psychologic techniques designed to diminish temporarily all forms of biologic stress, close to the minimum compatible with survival. Total elimination of stress—that is, cessation of demands made upon any part of the body, including cardiovascular, respiratory and nervous systems—would be the equivalent to death.[256]

Don't complain; change yourself. Meet new people, volunteer, take a part-time job. Don't ever act like death is coming soon because you don't know. I am ready for it now and living like it will never happen.

WE NOW KNOW how to live fully all the way to the end and how to leave gently. We can get ready now or not get ready and receive the default path provided by our modern medical system. The default only happens when we are passive, when we don't think about what we want and when we don't tell others what we want. I say, let's face the music and dance all the way out. I want to sing right along with Frank Sinatra, "I did it my way."

Want to join me?

Hattie

RESOURCES

THE FOLLOWING PAGES contain resources and an additional exercise to help you think beyond today to the legacy you want to leave.

CLIFF NOTES™ FOR LEAVING GENTLY

Here's the book in a nutshell. These are the steps to take to have some control over the decisions that must be made should your survival from illness be uncertain.

To do now:

1) **THINK.** Use the workbook section at the back of this book to guide your thinking about how you want your life to play out at the end.
2) **CHOOSE YOUR PROXY.** Your proxy is your healthcare power of attorney or surrogate or healthcare decision maker. These are words used to describe the person you select whom you feel will represent your (not their) wishes when you are no longer able to make decisions for yourself. The proxy can be your spouse, child, parent, friend: someone you trust to follow your wishes. Discuss your wishes with your proxy, your family, and your doctor. (Pages 102-108 provide more information on proxies.)

To do if you receive a serious diagnosis: Do 1 and 2 now, then these three steps.

1) **LEARN** as much as you can about your condition. Meet with your doctors to get answers about your illness, how serious it is, whether they thinks you will be alive by next year. They may or may not have answers; they may not have time or the skill to help you decide what to do. (Sample dialogues with doctors can be found on pages 81-85)
2) **ASK** for Palliative Care. This is a supporting team of healthcare professionals who can help you and your family recognize the seriousness of your health status, and are skilled in assisting you to make the necessary decisions when the outlook for your survival is in doubt. They provide support to your doctor to help relieve physical, emotional, spiritual, and socio-economic suffering, with teamwork of nurse, social worker, chaplain, and palliative physicians.
3) **WRITE** thank you notes and love letters. Take the trips you've always wanted to take. Eat the meals you want. Make the journey comfortable. Then smile and relax. Drink in the peace.

YOUR LEGACY

Please answer the following questions knowing that what you write can be the most meaningful gift you have ever given to the people you love. (When you finish writing, perhaps you would like to make a video or audio recording of these answers. Audio can be done easily on an iPhone using the Voice Memos app.)

How do you want to be remembered after you die? Imagine your son, daughter or friend telling someone who has never met you about your life.

What roles have you played in your life? Spouse, parent, volunteer, employee/business owner/bread winner, learner, explorer, friend, caregiver?

What stories should they know?

What lessons learned do you want to pass on to younger generations? These could be lessons from experience and from people including a spouse, children, friends or coworkers.

Who would you like to speak at a service honoring your life and what are your most important accomplishments that they could mention?

What are your hopes for the loved ones you leave behind?

What instructions would you like to give to them?

HATTIE'S HEALTHCARE DIRECTIVE
Let Nature Take Its Course

When I am not able to take care of myself I direct that medical care be withheld or withdrawn and that I be permitted to die naturally with only the administration of pain medications and other symptom-control medications to keep me comfortable.

Let nature take its course is my theme. I will do this myself, let nature take its course, when I am able to speak and manage then when I can no longer speak for myself, my trusted proxies will execute this plan.

My Trusted Decision-makers/Durable Power of Attorney
Hospice should be ordered by either a doctor who is on the case or accessed (a simple phone call) by a family member or either of my healthcare advocates who both have my durable power of attorney, Falyn Curtis or Dr. Pat Gary. If I have some sort of calamity in public, I realize that 911 will be called, CPR will get done to me if needed to keep me alive and I will get taken to an ER. Hopefully, very quickly after that my healthcare advocates will be contacted and they will implement this plan.

If I have a calamity at home, do not call 911. No healthcare provider, including EMTs, is allowed to touch me without consultation with Ms. Curtis or Dr. Gary. Dr. Gary said she would not let me die on the floor so I guess someone is allowed to pick me up off the floor and put me on a bed or sofa. Don't put me on the white sofas as you know things can get messy.

Forbidden Treatments/Override
I forbid and choose to forego CPR, surgery, chemotherapy, dialysis, tests, ventilation, feeding tubes (no tube down my nose and no percutaneous endoscopic gastrostomy tube), blood transfusions, antibiotics or IV hydration. I do not choose to die in a hospital or any other institution. The exception would be a Hospice in-patient facility due to the need for its pain and symptom management capabilities.

I authorize the withholding of artificially provided food, intravenous fluids, and other nourishments. If I cannot give directions regarding my medical care I intend for my family and physicians to honor this declaration as the final expression of my right to refuse medical care, food and water and I accept the consequences of that refusal.

No family member—my husband, my siblings, my nieces and nephews—may override this directive and no family member is in charge of my death and dying. I am in charge per these directives even if I have lost my mind (cognitive functioning), or my ability to communicate. My advocates agree they will follow this directive.

Comfort Care ONLY
A few more details to be very clear...

If I cannot feed myself, swallow, enjoy food, prepare simple meals, toilet myself, walk to my mailbox, (in healthcare-speak these are called the activities of daily living or ADL) recognize my family and friends, carry on a conversation, read, write emails and search the Internet, I want no more doctor's offices, no more hospitals, I will stop taking any medication (except to mitigate unpleasant symptoms such as pain, nausea, shortness of breath or agitation) and will not call 911.

This means, I may stop eating and drinking and do not want to be forced to eat or take water. I want Hospice to be in charge with Falyn Curtis and/or Dr. Gary (who both have my durable power of attorney) making sure that everyone sticks to this plan.

This means I should die within 7-10 days if I am a textbook case, however, experience teaches and experts say that it could take longer. It could take much longer as no one of us is in control. Don't worry about this because Hospice will be on the scene and you will not be alone. They have seen it all and will be a comfort to you.

If in the dying process I say I am changing my mind about all of this: do not listen and stick to this written plan.

If I can not speak for myself or if my mind—cognitive functioning—is gone, I forbid anyone to alter this directive and I repeat, do not force me to take in food or water. I have learned from palliative care nurses that feeding some people is painful to them so don't imagine that feeding me is loving me.

Feeding me is not loving me.

Not feeding me is not you killing me.

Not feeding me is letting nature takes its course.

Not feeding me is putting me fully, wholly and kindly into the hands of my God. I am ready to go back to God, I am ready to go home. You can hang up a sign that says, "SHE'S GOING HOME."

Then when I die, you can flip over the sign and it should read, "SHE'S GONE HOME."

Maybe Toni will make the sign.

Please realize that these instructions will be followed not based upon treatments starting or stopping, these instructions will be followed based upon how I choose to live out my last days. These instructions apply even if all I have is dementia. I do not want to be given any medical treatments or food or water when I reach the point I have described at the top of this page. Only provide palliative care with the help of hospice professionals.

If Bruce is still living and he doesn't want me to die in our bed or in our house, I understand that and I suppose Hospice has a bed for me somewhere.

Send Me Off in Song

I do hope you'll come and visit if you like but never feel that you have to and don't come because you feel guilty. Only come if you want to see how it is all working and if you have something to read to me or tell me.

Please play music...hymns, praise and worship songs, Opera Arias (No Wagner and only the big famous songs never the whole opera), all the famous symphonic works (No Mendelssohn and no Mozart as they bore me and I love the Russians). Play Bach anytime you don't know what else to play. No TV. Play Casting Crowns, Natalie Grant, Selah, David Phelps, Jason Crabb, and Michael English. At least once a day play my favorite song, "Give Me Jesus" performed by Fernando Ortega.

Have some fun! You can read the Psalms out loud but not the laments or the ones about being chased by enemies.

Thank you sweet ones. I am singing in my head, *Swing Down Chariot, Come and Let Me Ride* and *Angel Band.* You'll find these songs in my stack of CDs if you want to sing along.

My latest sun is sinking fast,
My race is nearly run
My strongest trials now are past
My triumph is begun

I know I'm nearing holy ranks
Of friends and kindred dear
I brush the dew of Jordan's banks
The crossing must be near

I've almost gained my heav'nly home
My spirit loudly sings
The holy ones behold they come
I hear the noise of wings

O come, angel band come and around me stand
O bear me away on your snowy wings to my immortal home
O bear me away on your snowy wings to my immortal home

FOR MY HEALTHCARE PROXY,
FAMILY, FRIENDS AND HEALTHCARE PROVIDERS
Durable Power of Attorney for Healthcare Decisions

You know from reading this document that if and when I can no longer speak for myself,

Falyn Curtis will be in charge of making sure that my wishes are respected. If this person is not available, the alternate proxy is **Dr. Pat Gary.**

I, **Hattie Bryant** being of sound mind, do hereby designate the above to serve as my Attorney-in-Fact, for the purpose of making medical treatment decisions for me (including the withholding or withdrawal of life-sustaining procedures, nutrition, hydration) if there is a time when I can no longer speak for myself. I understand the full import of this directive and I am emotionally and mentally competent to make this directive.

_____ *Hattie Bryant* _____ Date: *June 15, 2015*
Signature

Hattie Bryant has been personally known to me and I believe her to be of sound mind. In our joint presence, Hattie Bryant voluntarily dated and signed this writing.

Witness _____ *Larry Smith* _____ Date *June 15, 2015*

Witness Signature _____ *Larry Smith* _____

Address: _____ *10001 St. Peter Street* _____

City/State: _____ *New Orleans, LA* _____

Witness _____ *Sandy Smith* _____ Date *June 15, 2015*

Witness Signature _____ *Sandy Smith* _____

Address: _____ *10001 St. Peter Street* _____

City/State: _____ *New Orleans, LA* _____

SAMPLE POLST

Physician Orders for Life-Sustaining Treatment (POLST)

First follow these orders, then contact physician.
This is a Physician Order Sheet based on the person's current medical condition and wishes. Any section not completed implies full treatment for that section. A copy of the signed POLST form is legal and valid. POLST complements an Advance Directive and is not intended to replace that document. Everyone shall be treated with dignity and respect.

EMSA #111 B
(Effective 4/1/2011)

Patient Last Name:	Date Form Prepared:
Patient First Name:	Patient Date of Birth:
Patient Middle Name:	Medical Record #: *(optional)*

A

Check One

CARDIOPULMONARY RESUSCITATION (CPR): *If person has no pulse and is not breathing. When NOT in cardiopulmonary arrest, follow orders in Sections B and C.*

☐ **Attempt Resuscitation/CPR** (Selecting CPR in Section A **requires** selecting Full Treatment in Section B)
☐ **Do Not Attempt Resuscitation/DNR** (**A**llow **N**atural **D**eath)

B

Check One

MEDICAL INTERVENTIONS: *If person has pulse and/or is breathing.*

☐ **Comfort Measures Only** Relieve pain and suffering through the use of medication by any route, positioning, wound care and other measures. Use oxygen, suction and manual treatment of airway obstruction as needed for comfort. *Transfer to hospital **only** if comfort needs cannot be met in current location.*

☐ **Limited Additional Interventions** In addition to care described in Comfort Measures Only, use medical treatment, antibiotics, and IV fluids as indicated. Do not intubate. May use non-invasive positive airway pressure. Generally avoid intensive care.
    ☐ *Transfer to hospital **only** if comfort needs cannot be met in current location.*

☐ **Full Treatment** In addition to care described in Comfort Measures Only and Limited Additional Interventions, use intubation, advanced airway interventions, mechanical ventilation, and defibrillation/cardioversion as indicated. *Transfer to hospital if indicated. Includes intensive care.*

Additional Orders: _____
_____

C

Check One

ARTIFICIALLY ADMINISTERED NUTRITION: *Offer food by mouth if feasible and desired.*

☐ No artificial means of nutrition, including feeding tubes. Additional Orders:_____
☐ Trial period of artificial nutrition, including feeding tubes. _____
☐ Long-term artificial nutrition, including feeding tubes. _____

D

INFORMATION AND SIGNATURES:

Discussed with: ☐ Patient (Patient Has Capacity)   ☐ Legally Recognized Decisionmaker

☐ Advance Directive dated _____ available and reviewed →   Health Care Agent if named in Advance Directive:
☐ Advance Directive not available   Name: _____
☐ No Advance Directive   Phone: _____

Signature of Physician
My signature below indicates to the best of my knowledge that these orders are consistent with the person's medical condition and preferences.

Print Physician Name:	Physician Phone Number:	Physician License Number:
Physician Signature: *(required)*		Date:

Signature of Patient or Legally Recognized Decisionmaker
By signing this form, the legally recognized decisionmaker acknowledges that this request regarding resuscitative measures is consistent with the known desires of, and with the best interest of, the individual who is the subject of the form.

Print Name:	Relationship: *(write self if patient)*
Signature: *(required)*	Date:
Address:	Daytime Phone Number:	Evening Phone Number:

SEND FORM WITH PERSON WHENEVER TRANSFERRED OR DISCHARGED

HIPAA PERMITS DISCLOSURE OF POLST TO OTHER HEALTH CARE PROVIDERS AS NECESSARY

Patient Information

Name (last, first, middle):	Date of Birth:	Gender: **M F**

Health Care Provider Assisting with Form Preparation

Name:	Title:	Phone Number:

Additional Contact

Name:	Relationship to Patient:	Phone Number:

Directions for Health Care Provider

Completing POLST

- Completing a POLST form is voluntary. California law requires that a POLST form be followed by health care providers, and provides immunity to those who comply in good faith. In the hospital setting, a patient will be assessed by a physician who will issue appropriate orders.
- POLST does not replace the Advance Directive. When available, review the Advance Directive and POLST form to ensure consistency, and update forms appropriately to resolve any conflicts.
- POLST must be completed by a health care provider based on patient preferences and medical indications.
- A legally recognized decisionmaker may include a court-appointed conservator or guardian, agent designated in an Advance Directive, orally designated surrogate, spouse, registered domestic partner, parent of a minor, closest available relative, or person whom the patient's physician believes best knows what is in the patient's best interest and will make decisions in accordance with the patient's expressed wishes and values to the extent known.
- POLST must be signed by a physician and the patient or decisionmaker to be valid. Verbal orders are acceptable with follow-up signature by physician in accordance with facility/community policy.
- Certain medical conditions or treatments may prohibit a person from residing in a residential care facility for the elderly.
- If a translated form is used with patient or decisionmaker, attach it to the signed English POLST form.
- Use of original form is strongly encouraged. Photocopies and FAXes of signed POLST forms are legal and valid. A copy should be retained in patient's medical record, on Ultra Pink paper when possible.

Using POLST

- Any incomplete section of POLST implies full treatment for that section.

Section A:
- If found pulseless and not breathing, no defibrillator (including automated external defibrillators) or chest compressions should be used on a person who has chosen "Do Not Attempt Resuscitation."

Section B:
- When comfort cannot be achieved in the current setting, the person, including someone with "Comfort Measures Only," should be transferred to a setting able to provide comfort (e.g., treatment of a hip fracture).
- Non-invasive positive airway pressure includes continuous positive airway pressure (CPAP), bi-level positive airway pressure (BiPAP), and bag valve mask (BVM) assisted respirations.
- IV antibiotics and hydration generally are not "Comfort Measures."
- Treatment of dehydration prolongs life. If person desires IV fluids, indicate "Limited Interventions" or "Full Treatment."
- Depending on local EMS protocol, "Additional Orders" written in Section B may not be implemented by EMS personnel.

Reviewing POLST

It is recommended that POLST be reviewed periodically. Review is recommended when:
- The person is transferred from one care setting or care level to another, or
- There is a substantial change in the person's health status, or
- The person's treatment preferences change.

Modifying and Voiding POLST

- A patient with capacity can, at any time, request alternative treatment.
- A patient with capacity can, at any time, revoke a POLST by any means that indicates intent to revoke. It is recommended that revocation be documented by drawing a line through Sections A through D, writing "VOID" in large letters, and signing and dating this line.
- A legally recognized decisionmaker may request to modify the orders, in collaboration with the physician, based on the known desires of the individual or, if unknown, the individual's best interests.

This form is approved by the California Emergency Medical Services Authority in cooperation with the statewide POLST Task Force.
For more information or a copy of the form, visit **www.caPOLST.org**.

SEND FORM WITH PERSON WHENEVER TRANSFERRED OR DISCHARGED

GLOSSARY

ABBREVIATIONS:

AND allow natural death

CPR cardiopulmonary resuscitation

DNH do not hospitalize

DNI do not intubate

DNR do not resuscitate

DNAR do not attempt resuscitation

DPAHC durable power of attorney for healthcare

DPOA durable power of attorney

EHR electronic health record

G-tube gastrostomy tube

ICU intensive care unit

IV intravenous

MI myocardial infarction a.k.a heart attack

PCP primary care physician

PEG Percutaneous endoscopic gastrostomy - feeding tube

POLST Physician Order for Life-Sustaining Treatment

PVS persistent vegetative state

PSDA Patient Self Determination Act

TPN Total Parenteral Nutrition – intravenous feeding

VSED voluntarily stopped eating and drinking

ACUTE ILLNESS VS. CHRONIC CONDITIONS: Acute conditions are severe and sudden in onset. This could describe anything from a broken bone to an asthma attack. A chronic condition, by contrast, is a long-developing syndrome, such as osteoporosis or asthma. Note that osteoporosis, a chronic condition, may cause a broken bone, an acute condition. An acute asthma attack occurs in the midst of the chronic disease of asthma. Acute conditions, such as a first asthma attack, may lead to a chronic syndrome if untreated.[257]

ADVANCED CARE PLANNING: The whole process of discussion of end-of-life care, clarification of related values and goals, and embodiment of preferences through written documents and medical orders. This process can start at any time and be revisited periodically, but it becomes more focused as health status changes. Ideally, these conversations (1) occur with a person's healthcare agent and primary clinician, along with other members of the clinical team; (2) are recorded and updated as needed; and (3) allow for flexible decision making in the context of the patient's current medical situation.[258]

ADL OR ACTIVITIES OF DAILY LIVING: Healthy people are able to do the following activities without assistance. Bathing, dressing, grooming, oral care, toileting, transferring, walking, climbing stairs, eating, shopping, cooking, managing medications, using the phone, housework, doing laundry, driving, managing finances.[259]

ADVANCED DIRECTIVE: A broad term encompassing several types of patient-initiated documents especially living wills and documents that name a healthcare agent. People can complete these forms at any time and in any state of health that allows them to do so.[260]

AGENT: An individual designated in a legal document known as a power of attorney for healthcare to make a healthcare decision for the individual granting the power; also referred to in some statutes as durable power of attorney for healthcare (DPAHC), attorney in fact, proxy, or healthcare representative.[261]

ANOXIA: The absence, or near absence, of oxygen.

APNEA: Absence of breathing.

ARTIFICIAL NUTRITION AND HYDRATION: Artificial nutrition and hydration (or tube feeding) supplements or replaces ordinary eating and drinking by giving nutrients and fluids through a tube placed directly into the stomach (gastrostomy tube or G-tube), the upper intestine, or a vein.[262]

ASCITES: An abnormal accumulation of fluid within the abdomen. There are many causes of ascites, including non-functioning liver, cancer within the abdomen, congestive heart failure and tuberculosis.

BAG HER/HIM: To force air into lungs that are not functioning by placing a tight mask over the mouth and forcing air into it.[263]

BEREAVEMENT COORDINATOR: A bereavement coordinator monitors and manages services for people in mourning dealing with terminal illness or death. They act as the main manager of the volunteers, medical staff, and others who are working with the bereaved. These professionals can work in a variety of settings including hospice, nursing homes, hospitals, and home health.[264]

BRAIN DEATH: A permanent functional death of the centers in the brainstem that control breathing, heart rate, and other vital reflexes.[265]

BIOMARKER: Any measurable diagnostic indicator that is used to assess the risk or presence of disease.

BIOPSYCHOSOCIAL INTERVENTION: Interventions that systematically consider biological, psychological and social factors and their complex interactions to aid in the understanding of health, illness and healthcare delivery.[266]

CAPACITY TO MAKE A HEALTHCARE DECISION: An individual's ability to understand the significant benefits, risks, and alternatives to proposed healthcare and to make and communicate a healthcare decision. The term is frequently used interchangeably with competency but it is not the same. Competency is often distinguished as a legal status imposed by the court, although most states have dropped the term in favor of "legal incapacity."[267]

CARDIOPULMONARY RESUSCITATION (CPR): A group of treatments used when a person's heart and/or breathing stops. CPR is used in an attempt to restart the heart and breathing. It usually consists of mouth-to-mouth breathing or other method of ventilation and pressing on the chest to cause blood to circulate. Electric shock and drugs also are used used to restart or control the rhythm of the heart.[268]

CHRONIC PAIN: Ongoing or recurrent pain lasting beyond the usual course of acute illness or injury, or generally, more than 3 to 6 months and adversely affecting the individual's well-being.[269]

CODE BLUE: When a patient is in cardiopulmonary arrest and requires immediate medical intervention, this emergency is announced requiring medical professionals to rush to their specific location in order to perform immediate resuscitative efforts.

CONGESTIVE HEART FAILURE: Inability of the heart to keep up with the demands on it, with failure of the heart to pump blood with normal efficiency.

COGNITIVE FUNCTIONING: Basic cognitive functions include attention, working memory and long-term memory. Higher levels include speech and language, decision making, and executive control (planning, organization, coordination, implementation, and evaluation of many of our non-routine activities).[270]

COMA: A state of unrousable unconsciousness.

COMFORT CARE: Medical care that keeps you comfortable but makes no effort to treat an underlying disease. Choosing this means you take advantage of exit events. This allows nature to take its course; this is admitting that medicine is too small up against the force of nature. This is not assisted suicide. This is simply decreasing intervention and increasing comfort.[271]

CURATIVE CARE: Treatments that are focused on overcoming disease.

COMORBIDITIES: The co-existence of two or more diseases in the same person. For example, an obese person can have type 2 diabetes, sleep apnea, hypertension, heart disease, osteoarthritis and depression. Obesity is called the primary index diagnosis while the other conditions complicate the care.[272]

CHRONIC OBSTRUCTIVE PULMONARY DISEASE (COPD): A disease of adults, especially those over the age of forty-five with a history of smoking or inhalation of airborne pollution, characterized by airflow obstruction that is not fully reversible. The disease has features of emphysema, chronic bronchitis and asthmatic bronchitis.

DEATHBED BAGGAGE: These are imaginary suitcases which contain all the hurts, mistakes, failures, regrets, broken relationships, lies and bad behaviors that you engaged in which harmed yourself and others. This baggage was loaded full over your lifetime because you have tossed the problem into the bag(s) to get it out of your sight so you can ignore it. Imagine trying to lie down in peace then having heavy bags delivered to your bed and piled on top of you.

DIALYSIS: The clinical blood purification replacing the normal function the kidney performs.

DO NOT RESUSCITATE (DNR) ORDER: A physician's order written in a patient's medical record indicating that healthcare providers should not attempt CPR in the event of cardiac or respiratory arrest. In some regions, this order may be transferable between medical venues. Also called a No CPR order, DNAR (do not attempt resuscitation) order, and an AND (allow natural death) order.[273]

DRUG TOXICITY: The state of suffering ill effects from taking too much of a drug.

DURABLE POWER OF ATTORNEY FOR HEALTHCARE (DPAHC): Identifies the person (the healthcare agent) who should make medical decisions in case of a patient's incapacity.[274]

DYSPHAGIA: The action of swallowing is either difficult to perform or swallowed material seems to be held up in its passage to the stomach, often described by the patient as a sticking sensation.

ELECTROLYTE: A solution that produces ions (an ion is an atom or group of atoms that conduct electricity); for example, sodium chloride solution consists of free sodium and free chloride ions. In medical usage electrolyte usually means the ion itself; thus the term serum electrolyte level means the concentration of separate ions (sodium, potassium, chloride, bicarbonate, etc.) in the circulating blood. Concentrations of various electrolyte levels can be altered by many diseases.

EUTHANASIA: The act of taking life to relieve suffering.

EXIT EVENT: A naturally occurring illness that, if left untreated, will probably cause death. Pneumonia is a common potential exit event. Others are urinary tract infections, skin ulcers and infections, cardiac events, kidney failure, and simple dehydration.[275]

FASCICULATIONS: Involuntary contractions or twitching of groups of muscle fibers.

FRAILTY: Theoretically defined as a clinically recognizable state of increased vulnerability resulting from aging-associated decline in reserve and function across multiple physiologic systems such that the ability to cope with everyday or acute stressors is comprised. In the absence of a gold standard, frailty has been operationally defined by Fried et al. as meeting three out of five phenotypic criteria indicating compromised energetics: low grip strength, low energy, slowed waking speed, low physical activity, and/or unintentional weight loss.[276]

GRAND MAL SEIZURE: A generalized seizure characterized by loss of consciousness, often a fall to the ground, muscle rigidity, and then chronic muscle and limb twitching.

GUARDIAN: A judicially appointed guardian or conservator having authority to make a healthcare decision for an individual.[277]

HOSPICE: The word comes from the Latin word hospes which means to provide shelter for a guest. The term was first applied to the care of dying patients by Mme Jeanne Garnier who founded the Dames de Calaire in Lyon, France, in 1842. In 1982 Congress created a Medicare hospice benefit and this is what we tend to think of when we see the word. This benefit is a service delivered to homes, nursing homes, licensed facilities and hospitals which provides palliative care to a person who has a life-limiting condition who has six months or less to live. For those under sixty-five, most private third-party payers offer this benefit. An institution that provides a centralized program of palliative and supportive services to dying people and their families in the form of physical, psychological, social, and spiritual care; such services are provided by an interdisciplinary team of professionals and volunteers who are available in the home and in specialized inpatient settings.[278]

HYPOXIA: A deficiency of oxygen in the tissues.

HYPOXAEMIA: Respiratory failure.

INSTRUCTIONAL HEALTHCARE DIRECTIVE (ALSO REFERRED TO AS A LIVING WILL): A written directive describing preferences or goals for healthcare, or treatment preferences or willingness to tolerate health states, aimed at guiding future healthcare. In many states, the statutory directive is operative only when the individual lacks capacity and is diagnosed with a terminal condition, permanent unconsciousness, or other end-stage condition.[279]

INDIVIDUAL INSTRUCTIONS: An individual's direction concerning a healthcare decision. This may be written or verbal instructions describing goals for healthcare, treatment preferences, or willingness to tolerate future health states.[280]

INFORMED CONSENT: The principle that requires clinicians to provide sufficient information to patients or potential research participants in order to render their consent lawful.

INTUBATION: A shortened form of the term, "endotracheal intubation," the insertion of a tube through the mouth or nose into the trachea (windpipe) to create and maintain an open airway to assist breathing.[281]

LIFE SUSTAINING (LIFE SUPPORT) TREATMENT: Life sustaining treatment replaces or supports ailing bodily function. When people have treatable conditions, life support is used temporarily until the illness or disease can be stabilized and the body can resume normal functioning. At times, the body never regains the ability to function without life support or life-sustaining treatment. Some commonly used life-sustaining treatments are: CPR (cardiopulmonary resuscitation), intubation and mechanical ventilation, artificial hydration and nutrition, antibiotics and dialysis.[282]

LIVING WILL: A written, audio or video statement about the kind of medical care a person does or does not want under certain specific conditions if no longer able to express those wishes.[283]

MEDICALLY INDICATED TREATMENT: A way of saying it is appropriate or good for a certain condition. An antibiotic is said to be "indicated" for a bacterial infection if the antibiotic will treat that infection.[284]

MECHANICAL VENTILATION: Treatment in which a mechanical ventilator supports or replaces the function of the lungs. The ventilator is attached to a tube inserted in the nose or mouth and down into the windpipe (or trachea). Mechanical ventilation often is used to assist a person through a short-term problem or for prolonged periods in which irreversible respiratory failure exists due to injuries to the upper spinal cord or a progressive neurological disease.[285]

MINIMALLY CONSCIOUS STATE: A neurological state characterized by inconsistent but clearly discernible behavioral evidence of consciousness and distinguishable from a coma and a vegetative state by documenting the presence of specific behavioral features not found in either of these conditions. Patients may evolve to the minimally conscious state from coma or a vegetative state after acute brain injury, or it may result from degenerative or congenital nervous system disorders. This condition is often transient but may exist as a permanent outcome.[286]

MODERN MEDICINE: Some call this the Medical Industrial Complex. David Goldhill writes in his book *Catastrophic Care*, "In America there are approximately one million physicians in forty-one specialities, 5,754 hospitals, 12,751 FDA-approved prescription pharmaceuticals, and several hundred thousand Class III medical devices all treating 14,568 possible diagnoses in 310 million patients....Medicare sets six billion individual prices."[287]

Modern medicine for most of us starts with the physician who writes prescriptions and orders tests, who might send us to the hospital or to an assisted living place for rehab after an injury.

Think of nurses and other highly trained medical specialists. In 2012 there were 2.7 million Registered Nurses in the US. Modern medicine needs nurse practitioners, physical and occupational therapists, physician assistants, phlebotomists, clinical laboratory technicians, diagnostic medical stenographers, respiratory therapists, substance abuse counselors, epidemiologists, practical and licensed vocational nurses, medical assistants, medical equipment technicians, clinical social workers, medical secretaries, radiologic technologists, home health aides, personal care aides, surgical technologists, nursing aides, pharmacy technicians, paramedics, mental health counselors, and more. Think of all the buildings involved. This includes hospitals, doctor's offices, rehab facilities, out-patient clinics, nursing homes and long-term psychiatric residential treatment centers.

Think of drugs and medical devices. They are developed, they go through rigorous approval processes then are marketed to physicians and to us directly. Some refer to this part of modern medicine as Big Pharma. It is a nickname for the Pharmaceutical Research and Manufacturers of America which shortened is called, PhRMA. Big Pharma works hard to innovate, lobby congress, pay the fees associated with its regulating body, the US Food and Drug Administration (FDA), and to sell its ideas. The top 10 pharmaceutical companies in the world generated $462.8 billion in sales in 2011. The big US companies are Johnson & Johnson, Pfizer, Abbot Laboratories, Merck, Bristol-Myers Squibb and Eli Lilly.

Modern medicine has a very big budget. US Census Bureau reports in 2013:

- Healthcare Industry Annual Revenue Total: $1.668 Trillion
- Number of healthcare companies in the US: 784,626
- Number of healthcare company employees in the US: 16,792,074.

This source says that national health spending reached $2.8 trillion in 2012.[288]

MULTIPLE SYSTEM ORGAN FAILURE: More than one organ of the body stops working normally. Since each organ of the body has its own important purpose to keep us well, the more organs that don't work properly, the less likely it is that a patient will recover from a critical illness. Organs can stop working, or "fail," for a number of different reasons. Some common reasons that cause more than one organ at a time to fail are serious infections, low blood pressure (called "shock") and serious injuries (called "trauma"). In general, the chance of a patient dying in the hospital increases each day that organs don't improve functioning. (From personal conversation with Dr. Pat Gary, September 3, 2015.)

NASAL CANNULA: A small plastic tube that delivers oxygen through a person's nose.

NUREMBERG TRIALS: The trials took place in 1945 and 1946. Judges from the Allied powers presided over the hearings of twenty-two major Nazi criminals. These judges formulated the Nuremberg Code as a result of hearing Nazi doctors accused of conducting murderous and torturous human experiments in the concentration camps.[289] The Code influenced the Patient Self Determination Act of 1991 which gives patients the rights to direct their own care.

PALLIATIVE MEDICINE: Palliative medicine is the newest subspecialty of medicine. It was officially recognized by the American Board of Medical Specialties in 2006 and is unique as the care is delivered by an interprofessional team led by a physician or a nurse in consultation with a physician. A palliative care team includes physicians, nurses, dietitians, pharmacists, social workers, counselors, psychologists, chaplains and volunteers. Palliative medicine does not take the place of other physicians who are working with a patient—it adds a layer of care. Led by a physician or a nurse in consultation with a physician, the specially trained team supports other doctors, takes the time to know the patient and give the information needed to understand how serious problems might be. The palliative team is trained to listen well; manage difficult, resistant and distressing symptoms; provide care options, help with making choices; assist in grief/bereavement work; console for any spiritual pain and provide direction regarding financial needs.

Also called "comfort care," a comprehensive approach to treating serious illness that focuses on the physical, psychological, and spiritual needs of the patient. Its goal is to achieve the best quality of life available to the patient by relieving suffering, controlling pain and symptoms, and enabling the patient to achieve maximum functional capacity. Respect for the patient's culture, beliefs, and values is an essential component.[290]

PARACENTESIS: The process of drawing off fluid from a part of the body through a hollow needle or hollow tube.

PATIENT SELF-DETERMINATION ACT: An amendment to the Omnibus Budget Reconciliation Act of 1990, the law became effective December 1991 and requires most United States hospitals, nursing homes, hospice programs, home health agencies, and health maintenance organizations to give adult individuals, at the time of inpatient admission or enrollment, information about their rights under state laws governing advance directives, including: (1) the right to participate in and direct their own healthcare decisions; (2) the right to accept or refuse medical or surgical treatment; (3) the right to prepare an advance directive; and (4) information on the provider's policies governing use of these rights. The act prohibits institutions from discriminating against a patient who does not have an advance directive. The Patient Self-Determination Act further requires institutions to document patient information and provide ongoing community education on advance directives.[291]

PEG OR PERCUTANEOUS ENDOSCOPIC GASTROSTOMY: A procedure in which an opening is made into the stomach from the outside. It is usually done to allow food and fluid to be introduced into the stomach through a tube. Formerly a gastrostomy was always performed surgically, but it can now be done using an endoscope or by direct puncture and this is called PEG.

PERSISTENT VEGETATIVE STATE (PVS): A vegetative state is a clinical condition of complete unawareness of the self and the environment accompanied by sleep-wake cycles with either complete or partial preservation of hypotha-lamic and brainstem autonomic functions. The persistent vegetative state is a vegetative state present at one month after acute traumatic or non-traumatic brain injury, and present for at least one month in degenerative/metabolic disorders or developmental malformations. PVS can be diagnosed on clini-cal grounds with a high degree of medical certainty in most adult and pedi-atric patients after careful, repeated neurologic examinations by a physician competent in neurologic function assessment and diagnosis. A PVS patient becomes permanently vegetative when the diagnosis of irreversibility can be established with a high degree of clinical certainty (i.e., when the chance of regaining consciousness is considered exceedingly rare).[292]

POLYPHARMACY: The effects of taking multiple medications concurrently to manage coexisting health problems, such as diabetes and hypertension. Too often, polypharmacy becomes problematic such as when patients are prescribed too many medications by multiple healthcare providers working independently of each other. Also, drug interactions can occur if no single healthcare provider knows the patient's complete medication picture.[293]

PROXY: Substitute decision maker.[294]

PHYSICIAN-ASSISTED SUICIDE: The act of helping a patient to commit suicide by giving him or her the means (e.g. drugs) to do so. There are four states, Oregon, Vermont, California and Washington, where this is legal and one state, Montana, where it is legal with a court ruling.

POLST: The Physician Order for Life-Sustaining Treatment program, which began in Oregon, is a mechanism to elicit patients' care preferences, trans-late them into a set of medical orders addressing several high probability interventions relevant to the patient's current condition, document them on a highly visible form, and ensure their portability across care settings. Studies demonstrate the effectiveness of this program in translating preferences into care across selected settings.[295]

PHYSICIAN-PATIENT RELATIONSHIP: The physician we call "my doctor" will probably not be around when we are dying. According to the Accreditation Council for Graduate Medical Education, there are 140 medical subspecial-ties. The old fashioned idea of "sacred trust" between physician and patient has been gradually destroyed and we will not be able to depend upon one physician to direct our care. In a "multi-specialty care setting" we will prob-ably have a "care cooperative."[296]

RALE: An abnormal lung sound that can be heard through a stethoscope. This can mean there is fluid or infection in the lungs.

RESPIRATORY ARREST: Death or near death caused by cessation of breathing.

RESPIRATORY DISTRESS: Severe difficulty in achieving adequate oxygenation in spite of significant efforts to breathe.

SURROGATE: Proxy by default; a person who, by default, becomes the proxy decision maker for an individual who has no appointed agent.

SARCOPENIA: Loss of muscle mass due to aging.

SEPSIS: The putrefactive destruction of tissues by disease-causing bacteria or their toxins.

SINUS TACHYCARDIS: An increase in the heart rate above normal which may occur with exercise or excitement or it may be due to illness, such as fever.

TPN OR TOTAL PARENTERAL NUTRITION: Intravenous or IV nutrition. TPN supplies all daily nutritional requirements and can be used in the home or the hospital. TPN will drip through a needle or catheter placed in the vein for 10 to 12 hours, once a day or five times a week. TPN may include a combination of sugar and carbohydrates, proteins, lipids, electrolytes and trace elements, depending upon the needs of the patient.[297]

TRACHE OR TRACHEOTOMY OR A TRACHEOSTOMY: An opening surgically created through the neck into the trachea (windpipe) to allow direct access to the breathing tube and is commonly done in an operating room under general anesthesia. A tube is usually placed through this opening to provide an airway and to remove secretions from the lungs. Breathing is done through the tracheostomy tube rather than through the nose and mouth. The term "tracheotomy" refers to the incision into the trachea (windpipe) that forms a temporary or permanent opening, which is called a "tracheostomy," however; the terms are sometimes used interchangeably.[298]

TERMINAL: An incurable and irreversible condition caused by injury, disease, or illness that would cause death within a reasonable period of time in accordance with accepted medical standards, and where the application of life-sustaining treatment would serve only to prolong the process of dying.[299]

WITHHOLDING OR WITHDRAWING TREATMENT: Forgoing or discontinuing life-sustaining measures.[300]

ENDNOTES

1. Darlene Hunt and Jenny Bicks, "Musical Chairs," *The Big C.* Showtime. New York, NY: SHOW, 2011.

2. Sherwin Nuland, *How We Die: Reflections of Life's Final Chapter* (New York: Alfred A. Knopf Inc, 1994), 78.

3. Ibid., 259.

4. Mark Nepo, *The Book of Awakening: Having the Life You Want by Being Present to the Life You Have* (Massachusetts: Conari Press, 2000), 83.

5. The term "bad death" is personal. You decide for yourself what a good death or a bad death will be. In this book, I am using data that say most of us want a painless death and we want to be at home surrounded by our friends and family. This is what we all might call an old-fashioned, low-tech, good or a gentle death. Dr. Christine Cassel writes, "Today, although most people say they would prefer to die at home, 56 percent die in a hospital and 19 percent in nursing homes."

    Christine Cassel and Beth Demel, "Remembering Death: Public Policy in the USA," *Journal of the Royal Society of Medicine* 94 (2001): 433-436, accessed July 31, 2015, http://www.ncbi.nlm.nih.gov/pmc/articles/PMC1282180/.

6. At the front of this book I wrote about how I took this job seriously for myself when I watched my mom die.

7. These authors found, "Between 2000 and 2006, many elderly Americans needed decision making near the end-of-life at a time when most lacked the capacity to make decisions. The patients who had prepared advance directives received care that was strongly associated with their preferences. These findings support the continued use of advance directives."

    Maria J. Silveira, Scott Y.H. Kim, Kenneth M. Langa, "Advance Directives and Outcomes of Surrogate Decision Making before Death," *The New England Journal of Medicine* 362 (2010): 1211-1218, accessed July 31, 2015, http://www.nejm.org/doi/full/10.1056/NEJMsa0907901#t=article.

8. "At the end of life, patients are often unable to make their own medical decisions. Studies have estimated that surrogate decision-makers (hereafter referred to as surrogates) make approximately 75% of decisions for hospitalized patients with life threatening illness and 44–69% of decisions for nursing home residents. Moreover, geriatric patients with decision making capacity often elect to delegate decisions to their family or others."

    Elizabeth K. Vig et al., "Surviving Surrogate Decision-Making: What Helps and Hampers the Experience of Making Medical Decisions for Others," *Journal of General Internal Medicine* 22 (2007): 1274–1279, accessed July 31, 2015, doi: 10.1007/s11606-007-0252-y.

9. These physicians are concerned and working to find the best way to assess our competence. They write,

    Elderly patients with cognitive impairment and the clinicians who care for them face a challenge. These patients are at significant risk for having impaired decisional abilities. In this population with high medical comorbidity, the patients will face important

diagnostic and treatment decisions—decisions about where to live, and decisions related to planning for future incapacity.

"Our society's continued shifting of the responsibilities and burdens of medical decision-making toward the individual patient, in combination with the rapidly increasing number of elderly patients with dementia in our society, means that the need for accurate and efficient capacity evaluations will continue to increase."

S.Y. Kim, J.H.T. Karlawish and E.D. Caine, "Current state of research on decision-making competence of cognitively impaired elderly persons," *American Journal of Geriatric Psychiatry* 10 (2002): 151–165, accessed July 31, 2015, http://www.ncbi.nlm.nih.gov/pubmed/11925276.

[10] Michael Bean, "Death Probability Calculator," *Forio.com,* accessed July 31, 2015, http://forio.com/simulate/mbean/death-probability-calculator/overview/.

[11] "In the past century, medical and public health advances have almost doubled the average life expectancy, from less than 50 years to near 80. People who die in old age tend to experience a long period of functional decline before death, and thus require intensive caregiving and well-coordinated medical care. As medical advances allowed us to delay death, we moved death out of the home and into institutions."

Christine Cassel and Beth Demel, "Remembering Death: Public Policy in the USA," *Journal of the Royal Society of Medicine* 94 (2001): 433-436, accessed July 31, 2015, http://www.ncbi.nlm.nih.gov/pmc/articles/PMC1282180/.

[12] Barron Lerner, *The Good Doctors: A Father, a Son, and the Evolution of Medical Ethics* (Boston, MA: Beacon Press, 2015), 210.

[13] Joel Marcus, PsyD, interview with the author, Ochsner Cancer Center, Gayle & Tom Benson Center, New Orleans, November 22, 2013.

[14] Arialdi M. Minino, "Death in the United States, 2011," NCHS Data Brief (2013), accessed September 12, 2014, http://www.cdc.gov/nchs/data/databriefs/db115.pdf.

[15] Brian Skinner, "Your Body Wasn't Built to Last: A Lesson from Human Mortality Rates," Gravity and Levity (2009), accessed February 10, 2012, https://gravityandlevity.wordpress.com/2009/07/08/your-body-wasnt-built-to-last-a-lesson-from-human-mortality-rates/.

[16] K. Hawkes et al., "Human Actuarial Aging Increases Faster When Background Death Rates are Lower: A Consequence of Differential Heterogeneity?" *Evolution* (2012), 66:103-114, accessed January 20, 2014, doi: 10.1111/j.1558-5646.2011.01414.x.

[17] Dr. Carolyn McClanahan is a physician who practiced emergency medicine before she opened a financial planning firm. Dr. McClanahan writes for *Forbes* Magazine which is how I found her and she was kind to give me her insight into how doctors die, how she wants to die and how her family will know when it is time to let her go with only comfort care.

Dr. Carolyn McClanahan, telephone interview with author, August 5, 2014.

[18] Dr. Aaron Hagedorn, "Biology and Biomarkers of Aging," Lecture at USC Graduate School of Gerontology, Los Angeles, CA, March 4, 2014.

[19] Bob Fredericks and Post Wires, "Paralyzed Man Woken from Coma Chooses Death," *New York Post* (2013), accessed November 6, 2013, http://nypost.com/2013/11/06/man-chooses-to-end-life-after-fall-leaves-him-paralyzed/.

[20] "Deaths and Mortality," *Pub Center for Disease Control and Prevention* (2015), accessed February 15, 2015, http://www.cdc.gov/nchs/fastats/deaths.htm.

21 Scott A. Murray, "Interfacing palliative care with other disease specialties," lecture at Our Lady's Hospice Annual Conference—Moving Points in Palliative Care: Crossing Boundaries, Dublin, Ireland, March 4, 2010. Permission to use these charts was granted by Dr. Murray by personal communication September 18, 2014.

22 (1) Scott A. Murray et al., "Illness Trajectories and Palliative Care," *BMJ: British Medical Journal* 330 (2005): 1007-1011, accessed July 31, 2015, http://ncbi.nlm.nih.gov/pmc/articles/PMC557152. (2) Dr. Murray cites the trajectory work of June R. Lunney.

June R. Lunney et al., "Patterns of Functional Decline at the End of Life," *Journal of the American Medical Association* 289 (2003): 2387-2392, accessed July 31, 2015, doi:10.1001/jama.289.18.2387.

23 Dr. Ralph Corsetti, interview with the author, New Orleans, June 4, 2015.

24 Dr. Ulfers read an early manuscript offering edits and adding questions to the workbook. When I asked her for help I had no idea that Dr. McNulty (my mentor) had been one of her professors. He told me, "She is brilliant!"

Dr. Gretchen Ulfers, interview with the author in the author's home, September 1, 2014.

25 Dr. Michael Mitchell, "The Hospice and Palliative Care Physician," lecture at The USC Graduate School of Gerontology, Los Angeles, CA, September 25, 2014.

26 Dr. Kubler-Ross was a psychiatrist who discovered that her fellow physicians were not comfortable discussing death. From my reading I want to guess that this must have inspired her to do the difficult which was talk to dying patients then launch a new way of thinking about the dying process. While toward the end-of-life some would say she, "fell off the rails," that does not take away from the power of her first book that has been a guide for so many.

"Changing the Face of Medicine: Dr. Elizabeth Kubler-Ross," U.S. National Library of Medicine, accessed September 14, 2014, http://www.nlm.nih.gov/changingthefaceofmedicine/physicians/biography_189.html.

27 Elizabeth Kubler-Ross, *On Death and Dying: What the Dying Have to Teach Doctors, Nurses, Clergy and Their Own Families* (New York: Macmillian Company, 1969).

28 P.J. O'Rourke, *The Baby Boom: How It Got That Way* (New York: Atlantic Monthly Press, 2014), 226.

29 *The Wall Street Journal* reports that there is a "right-to-try" revolt. The opinion writers on February 9, 2015 said that "terminally ill patients" are fed up with slow FDA drug approvals.

"The Right-to-Try Revolt," *The Wall Street Journal* (2015), accessed July 31, 2015, http://www.wsj.com/articles/the-right-to-try-revolt-1423527365.

30 Laura Morrison, MD, FAAHPM is Associate Professor of Medicine (Geriatrics), Associate Clinical Professor of Nursing, Director of Palliative Medicine Education and Director, Hospice and Palliative Medicine Fellowship at Yale University. She is board-certified in Internal Medicine, Geriatric Medicine, and Hospice and Palliative Medicine and serves as an attending physician on the Yale-New Haven Hospital Palliative Care Consultation Service. I interviewed Dr. Morrison in Philadelphia at the 2015 Annual Assembly of the American Academy of Hospice and Palliative Medicine/Hospice and Palliative Medicine Nurses' Association.

Dr. Laura Morrison, interview with the author, Philadelphia, February 28, 2015.

31 Philippe Aries, "The Reversal of Death: Changes in Attitudes Toward Death in Western Societies," *American Quarterly* 26 (1974): 538. JSTOR (2711889). Accessed September 14, 2014, doi: 10.2307/2711889.

32 Ibid., 558.

[33] Dr. Fischer and I became friends in the fall of 1968 when we lived across the hall from each other our freshman year in college. I invited her to help us understand why we are so good at denying that death will come and this is what she told me. Her PhD is in Marriage and Family Therapy. She began her psychotherapy career working in pastoral counseling agencies in 1988 and has had a busy private practice since 2001.

Dr. Linda Fischer, telephone interview with the author, February 2, 2015.

[34] Camilla Zimmermann and Gary Rodin, "The Denial of Death Thesis: Sociological Critique and Implications for Palliative Care," *Palliative Medicine* 18 (2004): 121-128. EBSCOhost (12485419), accessed July 31, 2015, http://connection.ebscohost.com/c/articles/12485419/denial-death-thesis-sociological-critique-implications-palliative-care.

[35] Philippe Aries, "The Reversal of Death: Changes in Attitudes Toward Death in Western Societies," American Quarterly 26 (1974): 537. JSTOR (2711889).

Accessed September 14, 2014, doi: 10.2307/2711889.

[36] Geoffrey Gorer, "The Pornography of Death," *Encounter* (1955): 49-52, accessed September 15, 2014, http://www.romolocapuano.com/wp-content/uploads/2013/08/Gorer.pdf.

[37] Philippe Aries, "The Reversal of Death: Changes in Attitudes Toward Death in Western Societies," American Quarterly 26 (1974): 537. JSTOR (2711889). Accessed September 14, 2014, doi: 10.2307/2711889.

[38] While Herman Feifel estimated that 50,000,000 died in World War II, The National WWII Museum puts the total closer to 85,000,000.

"By the Numbers: World-Wide Deaths," The National WWII Museum, accessed March 5, 2015, http://www.nationalww2museum.org/learn/education/for-students/ww2-history/ww2-by-the-numbers/world-wide-deaths.html.

[39] Dr. Lamers is a psychiatrist who was involved in the development of hospice in the United States.

William M. Lamers, "Classics Revisited: Herman Feifel, *The Meaning of Death,*" *Mortality* 17 (2012): 64-78, accessed July 31, 2015, doi: 10.1080/13576275.2012.654709.

[40] Herman Feifel, *The Meaning of Death* (New York: McGraw-Hill, 1959), 121.

[41] William M. Lamers, "Classics Revisited: Herman Feifel, *The Meaning of Death,*" Mortality 17 (2012): 67, accessed July 31, 2015, doi 10.1080/13576275.2012.654709.

[42] Rick Warren, *What on Earth Am I Here For? The Purpose Driven Life* (Grand Rapids, MI: Zondervan, 2002), 162.

[43] This article summarizes points made by scholars in the fields of law, anthropology, neuroscience and literature at an April 22 symposium on medicalization—a phenomenon, they argued, that has infiltrated nearly every facet of modern life. The article quotes Christopher Lane, a literature professor at Northwestern University who defines medicalization as the term we use for "describing how common emotions and traits are turned into treatable conditions." The scholars in attendance also outlined the multiple societal forces that feed into the trend of medicalization: – the very existence of health insurance (costs are only reimbursable when associated with a definable medical condition) – death certificates (the need to name what caused a person's death – research funding (funding is more likely for problems defined as diseases) – drug trials and approval – and even a desire to wash one's hands of blame for one's condition (for instance, considering obesity a disease that assails people rather than the result, at least in part, of one's own actions and lifestyle).

"On the Medicalization of Our Culture," *Harvard Magazine* (2009), accessed August 2, 2015, http://harvardmagazine.com/2009/04/medicalization-of-our-culture.

44 Robert P. Watson and Dale Berger, "Reconsidering Ike's Health and Legacy: A Surprising Lesson in Duty at the Little White House Residential Retreat," *Eisenhower Institute*, accessed March 5, 2015, http://www.eisenhowerinstitute.org/publications/opinions__editorials/Watson_Berger_Reconsidering.dot.

45 Mark Salter, "Ike, D-Day and the Age of Accountable Leaders," *Real Clear Politics* (2011), accessed June 26, 2014, http://www.realclearpolitics.com/articles/2011/06/07/ikeday_and_the_age_of_accountable_leaders_110112.html.

46 Dr. Terry Simpson, a surgeon in Phoenix, strives to teach his patients how to cook. In one of his blogs he compares how President Eisenhower and President Johnson handled the news that they had high cholesterol. Eisenhower followed the rules of the day and was probably miserable while Johnson toward the end of his life must have said to himself, "Forget this. I'm going to eat what I want." Dr. Simpson makes this easy to understand when he writes, "For years America was told that saturated fat is bad for your heart. It was based on a faulty principle—that the fat in the arteries came from the fat in the blood which came from the fat in the diet. While it makes sense, it wasn't until after Johnson and Eisenhower died that science discovered that dietary fat contributes only a small amount to blood lipid levels. The idea was popularized by Ancel Keys."

Dr. Terry Simpson, "The Bad Fat isn't Bad and the Good Fat isn't Good," Your Doctor's Orders (2013), accessed July 31, 2015, http:// www.yourdoctorsorders.com/2013/03/the-bad-fat-isnt-bad-and-the-good-fat-isnt-good/.

47 Lois Pratt, "How Do Patients Learn about Disease?" *Social Problems* 4 (1956): 29-40. JSTOR (798565), accessed July 31, 2015, http://www.jstor.org/stable/798565.

48 Richard Sykes, "Penicillin: from Discovery to Product," *Bulletin of the World Health Organization* 79 (2001): 778-779, accessed July 31, 2015, http://www.who.int/bulletin/archives/79(8)778.pdf.

49 "Achievements in Public Health, 1900-1999: Control of Infectious Diseases," *Morbidity and Mortality Weekly Report* (MMWR), accessed June 19, 2014, http://www.cdc.gov/mmwr/preview/mmwrhtml/mm4829a1.htm.

50 George Rust et al., "Triangulating on Success: Innovation, Public Health, Medical Care, and Cause-Specific US Mortality Rates Over a Half Century 1950–2000," *American Journal of Public Health* 100 (2010): 95-104, accessed July 31, 2015, doi: 10.2105/AJPH.2009.164350.

51 Daniel Callahan, "Health Care Costs and Medical Technology," in *From Birth to Death and Bench to Clinic: The Hastings Center Bioethics Briefing Book for Journalists, Policymakers, and Campaigns*, ed, Mary Crowley (Garrison, NY: The Hastings Center, 2008), 79-82.

52 The average time it takes a cardiology team to clear a blocked artery is 64 minutes.

Harlan M. Krumholz et al., "Health Services and Outcomes Research: Improvements in Door-to-Balloon Time in the United States, 2005 to 2010," *American Heart Association Journals: Circulation* 124 (2011): accessed June 27, 2014, doi:10.1161/CIRCULATIONAHA.111.044107.

53 Elizabeth Chaitin, MSW, MA, DHCE, is the Director of Hospital Based Palliative Care for the Palliative and Supportive Institute of the University of Pittsburgh Medical Center. She is the author of many articles and the co-author of *Ethics and End-of-Life Decisions in Social Work Practice*. By the way, DHCE stands for Doctor of Health Care Ethics.

Dr. Elizabeth Chaitin, telephone interview with the author, October 31, 2013.

54 Shannon Brownlee, *Overtreated: Why too Much Medicine is Making us Sicker and Poorer* (New York: Bloomsbury, 2007), 78-79.

55 Richard Della Penna, MD, is a geriatrician and practiced medicine for 32 years. In addition to taking care of patients he served as Medical Director of the Kaiser Permanente Aging Network and the National Clinical Lead for Elder and Palliative Care which cared for nearly one million older adults. His clinical and care improvement activities have focused on depression, dementia, interdisciplinary team training, long term care, transitional care, and palliative care. He is a member of the Veteran Administration's National Geriatrics and Gerontology Advisory Commission and was on the Board of Directors of the National Alzheimer's Association from 2005 thru 2013. He is the 2010 recipient of UCLA's David H. Solomon Award, which recognizes influential leaders in the field of Geriatrics and today he is the Chief Medical Officer for Independa. I never could have imagined that when I met Richard in 1997 he would be a content expert for this book.

Dr. Richard Della Penna, telephone interview with the author, December 23, 2014.

56 Dr. De Georgia writes on page 676 that even though the concept of brain death was advanced in 1968, the boundary between death and life, "remains shadowy and vague...."

Michael A. De Georgia, "History of Brain Death as Death: 1968 to the present," *Journal of Critical Care* 29 (2014): 673-678, accessed July 31, 2015, doi: http://dx.doi.org/10.1016/j.jcrc.2014.04.015.

57 In his book, *Complications*, Dr. Atul Gawande says, "Medicine is, I have found, a strange and in many ways disturbing business. The stakes are high, the liberties taken tremendous. We drug people, put needles and tubes into them, manipulate their chemistry, biology and physics, lay them unconscious and open their bodies up to the world. We do so out of an abiding confidence in our know-how as a profession. What you find when you get in close, however— close enough to see the furrowed brows, the doubts and missteps, the failures as well as the success—is how messy, uncertain, and also surprising medicine turns out to be."

Atul Gawande, *Complications: A Surgeon's Notes on an Imperfect Science* (New York: Picador, 2003), 4.

58 This article was written by two distinguished psychologists who went to great effort to try to understand the answer to this question. There are many variables and all through the article you read the careful couching of findings such as, "dispositions may predispose individuals," "[v]ariables in the environmental and individual domains may affect disease," "[i]ndividuals who experience stress may be more susceptible to disease," "ratings may be influenced," "findings suggest that aspects of stress may play a difference role at different states of disease onset," "these women may have been particularly affected by adverse job characteristics," "The degree to which an individual is connected to others may also influence health." You see my point. It doesn't seem like we know why some people get sick and some people don't. There were a total of thirty-eight of these "may" statements in this thirty-page article. This is the way most academics report their findings because they know there are mysteries; they know the results are not perfect and that their methodologies may have some flaws. They are not like our grandmothers who say with certainty, "If you play outside in the snow without a jacket you'll get sick."

Nancy Adler and Karen Matthews, "Health Psychology: Why Do Some People Get Sick and Some Stay Well?" *Annual Review of Psychology,* 45 (1994): 229-259, doi:10.1146/annurev.ps.45.020194.001305. Accessed July 31, 2015.

59   Dr. Byock says in this excellent book, "We will encounter people whose lives we cannot save—diseases we cannot cure and injuries too grave to repair...."

Ira Byock, *The Best Care Possible: A Physician's Quest to Transform Care Through the End of Life* (New York: Penguin Group, 2012), 164.

60   Faulty science is part of the overselling of medicine. Hank Campbell wrote, "The Corruption of Peer Review is Harming Scientific Credibility," an opinion piece which appeared in *The Wall Street Journal*. In it he said, "In June, Dr. Francis Collins, director of the National Institutes of Health and responsible for $30 billion in annual government-funded research, held a meeting to discuss ways to ensure that more published scientific studies and results are accurate. According to a 2011 report in the monthly journal, Nature Reviews Drug Discovery, the results of two-thirds of 67 key studies analyzed by Bayer researchers from 2008-2010 couldn't be reproduced."

Hank Campbell, "The Corruption of Peer Review is Harming Scientific Credibility," *The Wall Street Journal* (2014), accessed July 14, 2014, http://www.wsj.com/articles/hank-campbell-the-corruption-of-peer-review-is-harming-scientific-credibility-1405290747.

61   Molly Billings, "The Influenza Pandemic of 1918," Stanford Online (2005), accessed July 31, 2015, http://virus.stanford.edu/uda/.

62   "The History of Vaccines," The College of Physicians of Philadelphia (2015), accessed July 31, 2015, http://www.historyofvaccines.org/content/timelines/polio.

63   "The Measles Vaccine," *The New York Times,* March 28, 1963.

64   Dan Munro, "Annual U.S. Healthcare Spending Hits $3.8 Trillion," *Forbes* (2014), accessed June 27, 2014, http://www.forbes.com/sites/danmunro/2014/02/02/annual-u-s-healthcarespending-hits-3-8-trillion/.

65   End-stage heart patients can get a ventricular assist device to keep them alive until they can get a heart transplant.

(1) Yukihiko Nosé, "Ventricular Assist Devices for Bridge to Myocardial Repair," *Artificial Organs* (2008) Vol. 32, No. 12, accessed July 31, 2015, doi: 10.1111/j.1525-1594.2008.00651.x.

(2) "Pipeline Embolization Device-P10018," U.S. Food and Drug Administration, accessed June 28, 2014, http://www.fda.gov/MedicalDevices/ProductsandMedicalProcedures/DeviceApprovalsandClearances/Recently-ApprovedDevices/ucm252130.htm.

(3) "FDA Approves Afrezza to Treat Diabetes," Drugs.com, accessed June 28, 2014, http://www.drugs.com/newdrugs/fda-approves-afrezza-diabetes-4050.html.

66   "One of the key ways of making healthy people believe they are sick is direct-to-consumer advertising of drugs and diseases."

Ray Moynihan and Alan Cassels, *Selling Sickness* (New York: Perseus Books Group, 2005), 12.

67   Welch et al., *Over-Diagnosed: Making People Sick in the Pursuit of Health* (Boston: Beacon Press, 2011), 180.

68   "The harm of over diagnosis to individuals and the cost to health systems is becoming ever clearer." Ms. Beck quotes Fiona Godless, editor in chief of the BMJ, as saying, "The harm of overdiagnosis to individuals and the cost to health systems is becoming ever clearer."

Melinda Beck, "It's Time to Rethink Early Cancer Detection," *The Wall Street Journal*, September 15, 2014.

69   "Our relentless search for wellness through medicine has created a kind of therapeutic imperative, the urge to treat every complaint, every deviation from the norm, as a medical condition."

Shannon Brownlee, *Overtreated: Why Too Much Medicine Is Making Us Sicker* and Poorer (New York: Bloomsbury USA, 2007), 2006.

[70] "Big Pharma and the Ethics of TV Advertising," (2013), accessed March 24, 2015, http://www.pharmaceutical-technology.com/features/feature-big-pharma-ethics-of-tv-advertising/.

[71] Nielsen considers the auto and financial sectors "big-spending advertisers" while they are 9.2% and 6.3% of spending at the same time Healthcare was at 11.3% in 2013.

Tracy Staton, "Pharma DTC ad spending sinks 11.5%, a $2B slide from 2006 peak," Fierce Pharma, last modified April 2, 2013, Accessed June 28, 2014, http://www.fiercepharma.com/story/pharmadtc-ad-spending-sinks-115-2b-slide-2006-peak/2013-04-02.

[72] "Peggy J. Wagner and Julia E. Hendrich are among researchers who report that approximately 50 percent of physician visits each year are for complaints with no organic explanation. A.G. Barsky and G.L. Klerman say that no serious medical disease is found in 30 to 60% of all visits to primary care physicians."

Judy Z. Segal, Health and the Rhetoric of Medicine (Illinois: Southern Illinois University Press, 2005).

[73] E.J. Topol, "Heart Facts," Cleveland Clinic Heart Book (2000), accessed July 9, 2014, http://my.clevelandclinic.org/services/heart/heart-blood-vessels/heart-facts.

[74] "Cracking the Code of Life," NOVA (2003), accessed July 9, 2014, http://www.pbs.org/wgbh/nova/genome/dna_sans.html.

[75] Heart and Vascular Institute, "Heart Facts," The George Washington University (2013), accessed July 31, 2015, http://www.gwheartandvascular.org/index.php/media-center/heart-facts/.

[76] Doris-Maria Vittingholf, "The First Fully Implantable Pacemaker," Siemens (2002), accessed July 9, 2014, https://www.siemens.com/history/en/news/1045_pacemaker.htm.

[77] Christiaan N. Barnard, "Human Cardiac Transplantation An Evaluation of the First Two Operations Performed at the Groote Schuur Hospital, Cape Town," American Journal of Cardiology, 22 (1968): 584-596.

[78] "Cardiopulmonary Resuscitation," American Family Physician 62, (7) (2000), accessed September 17, 2014, http://www.aafp.org/afp/2000/1001/p1564.html.

[79] John P. "Jack" McNulty, MD, FACP, FAAHPM, received a B.S. in Pharmacy in 1946 and graduated from Tulane University School of Medicine in 1951. He is board certified in Internal Medicine and in Hospice and Palliative Medicine. Although "retired," he still conducts seminars on palliative medicine for physicians and nurses.

Dr. Jack McNulty, interview with the author, Covington, LA, November 5, 2013.

[80] Maria Fidelis C. Manalo, MD, MSc., "Withholding and Withdrawing Life-Sustaining Treatment: Euthanasia or Acceptable Medical Practice?" FEU-NRMF Medical Journal 17 (2011): 68-78.

[81] In 1958 this same caring parent and physician, Dr. Safar, opened the first intensive care unit in the United States. When a man is up every night making sure his little one's lungs don't get so full of mucus that she can't breathe, it stands to reason that you want to invent a way to get her out of trouble. It follows that Dr. Safar was "the driving force behind modern ambulance services."

Anita Srikameswaran, "Dr. Peter Safar: A life devoted to cheating death," Post-Gazette (2014).

[82] Ibid.

[83] Dr. Barron Lerner, a medical historian, physician, writer and professor, delved into his father's detailed journals to understand more about what motivated his father's style of doctoring which was the norm for his generation. The result is a book that teaches us through the lives of these two men who saw medicine

change particularly around the ideas of paternalism and informed consent. The young doctor was shocked to learn that the patient his father had shielded from CPR did not have a "Do Not Resuscitate" instruction on file, thus the standard procedure would be to perform CPR.

Barron H. Lerner, "When the Doctor Knows Best," *The Wall Street Journal,* July 6, 2014.

[84] "'Good Doctor' Puts Past Medical Practices Under An Ethical Microscope," last modified May 13, 2014, accessed July 31, 2015, http://www.npr.org/2014/05/13/312169818/good-doctor-puts-past-medical-practices-under-an-ethical-microscope.

[85] Ancel Keys, "Diet and the Epidemiology of Coronary Heart Disease," *Journal of the American Medical Association.* 164 (1957): 1912.

[86] Stephen T. Sinatra MD et al., "The Saturated Fat, Cholesterol, and Statin Controversy: A Commentary," *Journal of the American College of Nutrition,* (2014) 33:1, 79-88, accessed July 31, 2015, DOI: 10.1080/07315724.2014.878633.

[87] 1977 Nutrient-based Goals:

- Increase consumption of complex carbohydrates and "naturally occurring sugars"
- Reduce consumption of refined and processed sugars, total fat, saturated fat, cholesterol and sodium.

Food-based Goals:

- Increase consumption of fruits, vegetables, and whole grains
- Decrease consumption of:
  - refined and processed sugars and foods high in such sugars;
  - foods high in total fat and animal fat, and partially replace saturated fats with polyunsaturated fats;
  - eggs, butterfat, and other high-cholesterol foods;
  - salt and foods high in salt; and
- choose low-fat and non-fat dairy products (except for young children).

"Dietary Guidelines for Americans 2010," United States Department of Agriculture Center for Nutrition Policy and Promotion, accessed July 2, 2014.

[88] Ibid.

[89] John Tierney, "Diet and Fat: A Severe Case of Mistaken Consensus," *The New York Times,* June 30, 2014.

[90] Researchers looked at twenty studies and found "our meta-analysis showed that there is in-sufficient evidence from prospective epidemiological studies to conclude that dietary saturated fat is associated with an increased risk of CHD (coronary heart disease), stroke, or CVD (cardiovascular disease)."

P.W. Siri-Tarino et al., "Meta-analysis of prospective cohort studies evaluating the association of saturated fat with cardiovascular disease," *American Society for Nutrition.* 91 (2010): 535-545.

[91] "As the 20th century closed, the Owl of Minerva finally stirred in the light of unavoidable evidence: None of this advice was preventing heart disease. What was left, as Ms. Teicholz adumbrates, was a monstrous thought: What if the crusade against cholesterol had fed the spread of obesity by encouraging a population to retreat from the very foods that would have satiated its hunger more efficiently than the hallowed grains and fruits and vegetables of the great dietary pyramid? What if the low-fat mantra had driven a population into feeling perpetually hungry? What if you were better off eating meat, eggs and dairy than a diet bloated in carbs and vegetable oils?"

Trevor Butterworth, "Book Review: 'The Big Fat Surprise' by Nina Teicholz" *The New York Times* (2014), accessed June 4, 2014, http://www.wsj.com/articles/book-review-the-big-fat-surprise-by-nina-techolz-1401923948.

[92] These authors tackle the 1977 guidelines and say in the opening paragraph, "Important aspects of the recommendations remain unproven."

A.H. Hite et al., "In the Face of Contradictory Evidence: Report of the Dietary Guidelines for Americans Committee," *Nutrition* (2010), 915-924.

93 Peter Whoriskey, "The U.S. Government is Poised to Withdraw Longstanding Warnings about Cholesterol," *The Washington Post* (2015), accessed July 31, 2015, http://www.washingtonpost.com/blogs/wonkblog/wp/2015/02/10/feds-poised-to-withdraw-longstanding-warnings-about-dietary-cholesterol/.

94 Paul J. Rosch, MD, "Why Reducing Stress is Much More Important than Lowering Cholesterol," *The American Institute of Stress Chairman's Blog* (2013), accessed May 12, 2014, http://www.stress.org/why-reducingstress-is-much-more-important-thanlowering-cholesterol/.

95 Scrubs Contributor, "An ER Nurse's Description of a Heart Attack," *The Nurse's Guide to Good Living,* (2011), accessed November 30, 2011, http://scrubsmag.com/er-nursesdescription-of-a-heart-attack/.

96 Nirav J. Mehta et al., "Cardiology's 10 Greatest Discoveries of the 20th Century," *Texas Heart Institute Journal* (2002), accessed July 31, 2015, http://www.ncbi.nlm.nih.gov/pmc/articles/PMC124754.

97 "Who Needs a Pacemaker?" *National Heart, Lung and Blood Institute* (2012), accessed July 31, 2015, http://www.nhlbi.nih.gov/health/health-topics/topics/pace/whoneeds.html.

98 "Implantable Cardioverter-defibrillators (ICDs)," Mayo Clinic, last modified July 16, 2015, accessed July 31, 2015, http://www.mayoclinic.org/tests-procedures/implantable-cardioverter-defibrillator/basics/definition/prc-20015079.

99 Dr. D.J. Birks, "Left Ventricular Assist Devices," *Heart* 96 (2010) 63-71.

100 These writers conclude that we should keep bringing on the statins. They say, "The 3-hydorxy-3-methylglutarate-CoA reductase inhibitors (statins) are the only class of drug widely used to lower cholesterol." "Statins work by blocking a liver enzyme needed to make cholesterol" according to Consumer Reports.

A bit of a miracle drug, this article also says, "Statins may also moderately reduce triglyceride levels, decrease inflammation in the arteries, and help raise HDL Levels." Doing what it does best, Consumer Reports gives pocket-book advice when it tells us, "All of our Best Buys— atorvastatin, lovastatin, pravastatin, and simvastatin—have been shown to reduce the risk of heart attack and deaths from heart attacks, and are available as inexpensive generics. You could save more than $100 per month if you pay out-of-pocket, and you opt for a generic instead of a brand name statin."

A. Shroufi and J.W. Powles, "Evidence-based public health policy and practice: Adherence and chemoprevention in major cardiovascular disease: a simulation study of the benefits of additional use of statins," *Journal of Epidemiology and Community Health* 64 (2010): 109-113.

101 Institute for Health Metrics and Evaluation, "Deaths from Cardiovascular Disease Increase Globally While Mortality Rates Decrease," *Science Daily* (2015), accessed July 23, 2015, http://www.sciencedaily.com/releases/2015/04/150402101410.htm.

102 In 2014 in the US, 29.1 million people or 9.3% of the population have diabetes. In 1958, 1.58 million people or 0.93% had diabetes.

Beverly Bird, "How Much Have Obesity Rates Risen Since 1950?" Livestrong.com (2013), accessed July 31, 2015, http://www.livestrong.com/article/384722-how-much-have-obesity-rates-risen-since-1950/.

103 Cancer Prevention Study II is an ongoing longitudinal study that began in 1982 involving 1.2 million men and women from fifty states, the District of Columbia and Puerto Rico.

Arthur Agatston, "Why America is Fatter and Sicker Than Ever," *Circulation Journal of the American Heart Association.* 126 (2012): 3-5.

[104] Sarah Knapton, "How Standing Might be the Best Anti-ageing Technique," *The Telegraph*, September 4, 2014.

[105] Miranda Prynne, "Stand up three hours a day for benefits of ten marathons, says top medic," *The Telegraph*, June 20, 2014.

[106] "The biological robustness in the neural substrates of sugar and sweet reward may be sufficient to explain why many people can have difficulty controlling the consumption of foods high in sugar when continuously exposed to them."

Serge Ahmed et al., "Current Opinion," *Clinical Nutrition & Metabolic Care* 16 (2013): 434-439.

[107] "Adult Obesity Facts," *Centers for Disease Control and Prevention* (2015), accessed July 31, 2015, http://www.cdc.gov/obesity/data/adult.html.

[108] Richard J. Johnson, MD and Timothy Gower, *The Sugar Fix: The High-Fructose Fallout That is Making You Fat and Sick* (New York: Simon & Schuster, 2008), 43.

[109] "The History of Cancer," American Cancer Society (2014), accessed July 31, 2015, http://www.cancer.org/acs/groups/cid/documents/webcontent/002048-pdf.pdf.

[110] "The 1971 National Cancer Act: Investment in the Future," National Institute of Health (1997), accessed July 31, 2015, http://www.nih.gov/news/pr/mar97/nci-26c.htm.

[111] H. Gilbert Welch, Lisa M. Schwartz and Steven Woloshin, *Over-Diagnosed, Making People Sick in the Pursuit of Health*, (Boston: Beacon Press, 2011), 180.

[112] Ibid., 47.

[113] Ibid., 53.

[114] Anthony B. Miller et al., "Twenty-five year follow-up for breast cancer incidence and mortality of the Canadian National Breast Screening Study: randomised screening trial," *The BMJ* (2014), accessed July 31, 2015, http://www.bmj.com/content/348/bmj.g366.

[115] Charles F. von Gunten, MD, PhD, is Vice President, Medical Affairs, Hospice and Palliative Medicine for OhioHeath. He is known for developing an early model of hospital-based palliative care and has played a lead role in the developing and achieving formal recognition of the sub-specialty of palliative medicine. He is the Editor-in-Chief of the Journal of Palliative Medicine, the journal of record for palliative medicine. Dr. von Gunten is the Chairman, Test Committee, Hospice & Palliative Medicine, American Board of Medical Specialties. He is the past President of the American Association for Cancer Education and the Co-Principal for the Education for Physicians on End-of-life Care (EPEC) Project and its revision for oncology, EPEC-O. He received a life-time achievement award from the American Academy for Hospice and Palliative Medicine in 2011 when he was only fifty-four years old. Dr. von Gunten earned a PhD in Biochemistry and his medical degree with honors from the University of Colorado Health Sciences Center in 1988. He did residency in Internal Medicine and Hematology/Oncology at the McGaw Medical Center of Northwestern University in Chicago.

Dr. Charles von Gunten, e-mail message to the author, June 14, 2015

[116] Daniel Matlock, MD, MPH, is on the faculty of the University of Denver Department of Medicine. He is an internist who has focused much of his attention on palliative medicine. He is the principle investigator for a pilot randomized trial of a decision aid designed to assist with advance care planning on the inpatient palliative care service at the University of Colorado Hospital.

Dr. Daniel Matlock, e-mail message to author, June 14, 2015.

[117] Dr. Jack McNulty, e-mail message to author, June 14, 2015.

[118] C. Lee Ventola, "Direct-to-Consumer Pharmaceutical Advertising," *Pharmacy and Therapeutics* 36 (2010): 2, accessed June 18, 2014, http://www.ncbi.nlm.nih.gov/pmc/articles/PMC3278148/#!po=58.3333.

[119] "US prescription sales were up 3.2% in 2013," *Pharmaceutical Commerce* (2014), accessed June 18, 2014, http://www.pharmaceuticalcommerce.com/index.php?pg=business_finance&articleid=27220.

[120] Christian Torres, "Report: Health Care Costs to Reach Nearly One-Fifth of GDP by 2021," *Kaiser Health News* (2012), accessed June 18, 2014, http://khn.org/news/report-health-spending-will-climb-to-nearly-one-fifth-of-gdp/.

[121] "Popping Pills: Prescription Drug Abuse in America," National Institute on Drug Abuse (2014), accessed July 23, 2015,http://www.drugabuse.gov/related-topics/trends-statistics/infographics/popping-pills-prescription-drug-abuse-in-america.

[122] Allison McCabe, "America's Number One Prescription Sleep Aid Could Trigger 'Zombies,' Murder and Other Disturbing Behaviour," *Alternet* (2014), accessed July 31, 2015, http://www.alternet.org/drugs/americas-number-one-prescription-sleep-aid-could-trigger-zombies-murder-and-other-disturbing.

[123] The National Institutes of Health medical research budget for 2014 is $30.1 billion.

"NIH Budget," National Institutes of Health, accessed June 27, 2014, http://www.nih.gov/about/budget.htm.

[124] Biomedical research and development expenditures in 2012 in the US were $119.3 billion. $48.9 billion of public money and $70.4 billion of private money.

Justin Chakma, B.Sc. et al., "Asia's Ascent – Global Trends in Biomedical R&D Expenditures" *New England Journal of Medicine* 370 (2014): 3-6.

[125] "U.S. Investment in Health Research: 2012 reports that private industry spent $69 Billion on medical research and development in 2012," *Research America*, accessed June 29, 2014, http://www.researchamerica.org/sites/default/files/uploads/healthdollar10.pdf.

[126] William J. Broad, "Billionaires With Big Ideas Are Privatizing American Science," *The New York Times* (2014), accessed June 27, 2014, http://www.nytimes.com/2014/03/16/science/billionaires-with-big-ideas-are-privatizing-american-science.html.

[127] E.R. Dorsey et al., "Funding of US Biomedical Research, 2003-2008," *Journal of the American Medical Association* 3030 (2010): 137-143.

[128] "In 2011, U.S. Charitable giving totaled $298.4 billion, a 4% increase, and the second year to see an increase following two years of declines. One fact that continues to be noteworthy year after year is that the majority of giving in our country continues to come from individuals. Of the $298.42 billion given in 2011, 88% came from individuals when combining bequests and individual and family foundation giving." This data does not tell us what percentage of the individual gifts go to medical research. I only cite this to make the point that Americans give of their own hard-earned money to many good causes and we know some are giving enough to get their names on buildings which deliver healthcare. Just one of these generous souls was business man, Monroe Dunaway Anderson, whose foundation gave $500,000 in 1941 to build what we now know as the MD Anderson Cancer Center.

"Giving USA 2012 Snapshot," *Focus on Philanthropy Blog* (2012), accessed July 31, 2015.

[129] Dr. Laura Morrison, interview with the author, Philadelphia, February 28, 2015.

[130] H. Gilbert Welch, Lisa M. Schwartz and Steven Woloshin, *Over-Diagnosed, Making People Sick in the Pursuit of Health* (Boston: Beacon Press, 2011).

131 The authors deliver a blow to the activity of redefining disease as they say, "Finally, it is important to acknowledge that there are strong financial motivations to expand disease definitions. Whether or not it is in the patient's best interest, expanded disease definitions mean larger markets for pharmaceuticals. It is worth noting that the WHO study group—the group responsible for the current definition of osteoporosis— was funded by three drug companies: Rorer, Sandoz and SmithKline Beecham." M. Brooke Herndon et al., "Implications of Expanding Disease Definitions: The Case of Osteoporosis," *Health Affairs* 26 (2007): 1702-1711, accessed November 2014, doi: 10.1377/hlthaff.26.6.1702.

132 H. Gilbert Welch, Lisa M. Schwartz and Steven Woloshin, *Over-Diagnosed, Making People Sick in the Pursuit of Health* (Boston: Beacon Press, 2011).

133 Linda A. Johnson, "Against Odds, Lipitor Becomes World's Top Seller," *USA Today* (2011), accessed August 7, 2015, http://usatoday30.usatoday.com/ news/health/medical/health/medical/ treatments/story/2011-12-28/Against- odds-Lipitor-became-worlds-top- seller/52250720/1.

It is fitting that Robert Field begins his discussion about the market dynamics of the prescription drugs business with the story of Lipitor.

Robert I. Field, *Mother of Invention: How the Government Created Free-Market Health Care*, (New York: Oxford University Press, 2014), 1.

134 Heidi Ledford "Cholesterol limits lose their lustre," last modified March 8, 2013, http://www.nature.com/news/choles- terol-limits-lose-their-lustre-1.12509.

135 Ibid.

136 Shannon Brownlee, *Overtreated: Why Too Much Medicine Is Making Us Sicker and Poorer* (New York: Bloomsbury USA, 2007), 2006.

137 Ken Murray, "How Doctors Die," *Zócalo* (2011) accessed December 3, 2011, http://www.zocalopublicsquare. org/2011/11/30/how-doctors-die/ideas/ nexus/.

138 Sherwin Nuland, *How We Die: Reflections on Life's Final Chapter* (New York: Alfred A. Knopf Inc, 1994), 207.

139 Dr. John B. Cazale is an orthopedic surgeon who received his medical degree from Louisiana State University School of Medicine in 1973. He completed his internship at Charity Hospital and his residency at the Tulane Medical School Hospital.

Dr. John Cazale, interview with the author at the author's home, New Orleans, May 17, 2014.

140 Atul Gawande, *Being Mortal* (New York: Penguin, 2014), 35.

141 Dr. Pat Gary received her doctor of medicine from Tulane University School of Medicine in New Orleans in 1974. She completed a General Surgery Residency at Alameda County General Hospital in Oakland, California and is board-certified by the American Board of Emergency Medicine. After decades of work in emergency medicine, today she works in primary care. Dr. Gary is a close personal friend who has served as the "voice of reason" for this book. She gave me many interviews. Some took place in my home, some in her home, one on a long drive we took across the state, some on the telephone and she has even text-ed me the answers to questions.

Dr. Pat Gary, interview with the author at the author's home, New Orleans, May 18, 2014.

142 Martin Scurr, "Why MOST Doctors Like Me Would Rather DIE Than Endure the Pain of Treatment We Inflict On Other's for Terminal Diseases," *Daily Mail*, February 14, 2012.

143 Ann Neumann, "Dying with Class," in Ron Scapp, *Living With Class: Philosophical Reflections on Identity and Material Culture* (New York: Palgrave Macmillan, 2013), 109.

[144] Carolyn McClanahan, MD, "Doctors Do Die Differently - How We Make Certain," *Forbes* (2015), accessed May 21, 2012, http://www.forbes.com/sites/carolyn-mcclanahan/2012/03/02/doctors-do-die-differently-how-we-make-certain/.

[145] Dr. Barron Lerner writes, "My father believed that many well-meaning physicians and hospitals had lost sight of the basic human gesture of allowing a person to die in peace free from suffering." Dr. Lerner reports that his father ensured gentle end-of-life care for several of his elderly family members hinting that the senior Dr. Lerner saw no reason to prolong death.

Barron Lerner, *The Good Doctor* (Boston: Beacon Press, 2014), 113.

[146] In a personal interview with a hospital social worker, who must remain anonymous, I learned that one of the busiest neurosurgeons in her hospital "allowed a gentle passing" for a sibling who had suffered a brain injury. The social worker was only sad that the same surgeon was not able to allow this for others because of course surgeons are required to discuss cases with families and receive consent. We don't know if the same surgeon is reticent to engage families or if in general families are afraid to let loved ones go. We do know that the family member of the surgeon was treated differently than other patients. In this case, one surgeon saw the damage and let his sibling go.

Anonymous, interview with the author, Louisiana, May 28, 2013.

[147] Amy E. Liepert et al., "Surgery at the End of Life: For Love or Money?" *Bulletin of the American College of Surgeons* (2012), accessed July 31, 2015, http:// bulletin.facs.org/2012/08/surgery-at-the-end-of-life-for-love-or-money/#.

[148] Shannon Brownlee, "What Doctors Know—and We Can Learn—About Dying," *TIME* (2015), accessed May 9, 2015, http://ideas.time.com/2012/01/16/what-doctorsknow-and-we-can-learn-about-dying/.

[149] J.J. Gallo et al., "Life-Sustaining Treatments: What Do Physicians Want and Do They Express Their Wishes to Others?" *Journal of the American Geriatrics Society* 51 (2003): 961-969.

[150] Anita Brikman, "Lack of Awareness Continues to be a Barrier for Americans in Making Medical Wishes Known," *National Hospice and Palliative Care Organization* (2013), accessed July 31, 2015, http://www.nhpco.org/press-room/press-releases/new-study-advance-directives.

[151] Angelo Volandes, *The Conversation: A Revolutionary Plan for End-of-Life Care* (New York: Bloomsbury Press, 2015), 9.

[152] J.J. Gallo et al., "Stability of Preferences for End-of-Life Treatment After 3 Years of Follow-Up," *JAMA Internal Medicine* 168 No. 19 (2008): 2125-2130.

[153] Joseph Gallo, interview with the author, Baltimore, MD, March 21, 2015.

[154] J.B. Straton et al., "Physical Preferences for Treatment at the End of Life: The Jophns Hopkins Precursors Study," *The Journal of the American Geriatrics Society* 52 (2004): 577-582.

[155] J.J. Gallo et al., "Stability of Preferences for End-of-Life Treatment After 3 Years of Follow-Up," *JAMA Internal Medicine* 168, no. 19 (2008): 2125-2130.

[156] Joseph Gallo is a professor at Johns Hopkins Bloomberg School of Public Health.

Joseph Gallo, interview with the author, Baltimore, MD, March 21, 2015.

[157] H. Kramer et al., "Do Unto Others: Doctors' Personal End-of-Life Resuscitation Preferences and Their Attitudes toward Advance Directives," *PLOS One* accessed June 3, 2014, doi. 10.1371/journal.pone.0098246.

[158] E.J. Emanuel, "Why I Hope to Die at 75, An Argument the Society and Families – and You – Will be Better Off if Nature Takes Its Course Swiftly and Promptly," *The Atlantic* (2014), accessed July 31, 2015, http://www.theatlantic.com/features/archive/2014/09/why-i-hope-to-die-at-75/379329/.

159 Eileen M. Fitzpatrick and Jeanne Fitzpatrick, *A Better Way of Dying: How to Make the Best Choices at the End of Life (Why Your Living Will is Not Enough,* (New York: Penguin Books, 2010), 157.

160 L.M. Jacobs et al., "Trauma Death, View of the Public and Trauma Professionals on Death and Dying from Injuries," *JAMA Surgery* 143, no. 8 (2008): 730-735.

161 Dr. David Treen, interview with the author, Tulane School of Medicine, New Orleans, LA, May 19, 2014.

162 "Video Affects End-of-Life Decisions," Harvard Medical School (2012), accessed July 31, 2015, http://hms.harvard.edu/news/video-affects-end-life-decisions-12-10-12.

163 "Angelo Volandes, MD," ACP Decisions, accessed October 7, 2014, http://www.acpdecisions.org/about/.

164 "Medical Professionalism in the New Millennium: A Physician Charter, Project of the ABIM Foundation, ACP-ASIM Foundation and European Federations of Internal Medicine," *Annals of Internal Medicine* 135, no. 3 (2002): 243-246.

165 E.G. Campbell et al., "Survey Shows that At Least Some Physicians are not Always Open or Honest With Patients," *Health Affairs* 31, no. 2 (2012): 383-391.

166 "Delivering High-Quality Cancer Care: Charting a New Course for a System in Crisis," The National Academies of Science (2013), accessed May 21, 2014, http://iom.nationalacademies.org/Reports/2013/Delivering-High-Quality-Cancer-Care-Charting-a-New-Course-for-a-System-in-Crisis/Videos.aspx.

167 Dr. Daniel Matlock, email message to the author, June 14, 2015.

168 Maggie Mahar, "Breast Cancer: Catching Up with Amy Berman, a Woman Who Chose Life Over Longevity," Health Beat (2013), accessed May 6, 2014, http://www.healthbeatblog.com/2013/10/breast-cancer-catching-up-with-amy-berman-a-woman-who-chose-life-over-longevity-2/.

169 Clifton Leaf, "Why We're Losing the War on Cancer and How to Win it," *CNN* (2007), accessed July 31, 2015, http://www.cnn.com/2007/HEALTH/01/09/fortune.leaf. waroncancer/index.html.

170 Laura Landro, "Book Review: 'The Truth in Small Doses' by Clifton Leaf- 'The Cancer Chronicles' by George Johnson," *The Wall Street Journal* (2013), accessed May 10, 2014, http://online.wsj.com/news/articles/SB 1000142412788732363 970457901277289 3323140.

171 This study revealed that 86% of the physicians who participated knew patients were close to death but only 11% talked with the patient about the possibility that death was coming soon.

C. Schulz et al., "Evaluating an Evidence-Based Curriculum in Undergraduate Palliative Care Education: Piloting a Phase II Exploratory Trial for a Complex Intervention," *BMC Medical Education,* 13, 1 (2013) accessed July 31, 2015, doi:10.1186/1472-6920-13-1.

172 Dr. Chaitin and others who have worked in hospitals for decades say things like, "In a hospital setting we see families in crises and doctors in training. Young doctors don't know what to say, how much or little to say and this results in confusion." If the patient is a doctor there is probably not much confusion. The patient himself or herself can sort things out and thus has a better chance of getting the kind of care they want.

Dr. Elizabeth Chaitin, telephone interview with the author, October 31, 2014.

173 Dr. Gawande writes when meeting with an oncologist about chemotherapy options for his father, "the discussion became difficult for me or my parents to follow, despite all three of us being doctors."

Atul Gawande, *Being Mortal* (New York: Penguin 2014), 218.

174 This list of expressions and the meanings were edited by Dr. Pat Gary and Dr. Joan Harrold. I met Dr. Harrold over breakfast at a medical meeting. At that brief encounter I told her I was writing a book and asked if she would give me an interview. She didn't hesitate to say yes. Later, I discovered that she is the co-author of the very important book, *Handbook for Mortals: Guidance for People Facing Serious Illness.* I regret not knowing who was standing next to me at the time. If I had known then what I know now I would have told her, "Thank you for your decades of commitment to medicine and palliative care." These are the letters you find behind her name: MD, MPH, FAAHPM, FACP. During her Cancer Prevention and Control Fellowship at the National Cancer Institute, she completed a Master of Public Health degree with special emphasis in epidemiology and biostatistics. Dr. Harrold is a past member of the Board of Directors of the American Academy of Hospice and Palliative Medicine (AAHPM) and is a past section leader of the Physician Section of the National Council of Hospice and Palliative Professionals of the National Hospice and Palliative Care Organization (NHPCO). She is a member of the Examination Committee for Hospice and Palliative Medicine under the auspices of the American Board of Internal Medicine. She also is a past President of the Board of Directors of the Pennsylvania Hospice Network and continues to serve on the board. Dr. Harrold is the Medical Director and Vice President, Medical Services of Hospice & Community Care and is board certified in Internal Medicine and Hospice and Palliative Medicine.

Dr. Pat Gary, interview with the author, New Orleans, LA, May 9, 2014.

Dr. Joan Harrold, telephone interview with the author, July 18, 2014.

175 Dr. Robert Arnold and his colleagues teach other physicians the ask-tell-ask method of communication. Ask the patient why they are in the office and what they understand about their current situation. Tell the patient the truth then ask the patient what they just heard the doctor say. We can't die like a doctor because we don't understand what they understand when they hear a diagnosis. We must work to demand the truth that will give us in the last years of our life what we want not what they want for us or what we get because we didn't dig hard enough to get to the truth.

A.L. Back et al., "Approaching Difficult Communication Tasks in Oncology," *CA: A Cancer Journal for Clinicians* 55, no. 3, (2005), 164–177, accessed July 31, 2015, doi: 10.3322/canjclin.55.3.164.

176 Kevin B. O'Reilly, "Checklist Approach to be Tested in End-of-Life Care Planning," *American Medical News* (2012), accessed July 31, 2015, http://amednews.com/article/20120613/profession/306139996/8/.

177 Dominick L. Frosch et al., "Authoritarian Physicians and Patients' Fear of Being Labeled 'Difficult' Among Many Key Obstacles to Shared Decision Making," *Health Affairs* 31, no. 5 (2012): 1030-1038.

178 "Amount of Time U.S. Primary Care Physicians Spent with Each Patient as of 2014," *Statista* (2014), accessed August 3, 2015, http://www.statista.com/statistics/250219/us-physicians-opinion-about-their-compensation/.

179 Dr. Elizabeth Chaitin taught me that I can fire any physician who won't work with me to get a palliative care consultation.

Dr. Elizabeth Chaitin, telephone interview with the author, January 6, 2015.

180 Dr. Richard Della Penna, telephone interview with the author, December 23, 2014.

181 Sherwin Nuland, *How We Die: Reflections of Life's Final Chapter* (New York: Alfred A. Knopf Inc, 1994), 143.

[182] Dr. Laura Morrison, interview with the author, Philadelphia, February 28, 2015.

[183] Dr. Aboderin makes the strong point that in every society throughout history, filial obligation is, "enshrined in moral or religious code be they Indigenous, Judeo-Christian, Confucian, Islamic, Buddhist or otherwise."

Isabella Aboderin, "Conditionality and Limits of Filial Obligation," *Oxford Institute of Ageing Working Papers* (2005), accessed July 31, 2015, http:www.ageing.ox.ac.uk.

[184] Writing for the *Journal of Family Nursing,* researchers report that older adults do not want to be a burden or a bother or a worry to friends and family. The older adults see that their adult children have busy complicated lives and don't want to add to anyone's "to do" list.

H.R. Bogner et al., "You Don't Want to Burden Them: Older Adults' View of Family Involvement in Care," *Journal of Family Nursing* (2007), accessed July 31, 2015, doi: 10.1177/1074840709337247.

[185] Rose M. Kreider et al., "America's Families and Living Arrangements: 2012," *United States Census Bureau* (2013), accessed May 2, 2014, http://www.census. gov/prod/2013pubs/p20-570.pdf.

[186] "A Profile of Older Americans: 2011," *US Administration on Aging* (2012), accessed May 2, 2014, http://www.aoa. gov/Aging_Statistics/Profile/2011/6.aspx.

[187] H.R. Bogner et al., "You Don't Want to Burden Them: Older Adults' Views on Family Involvement in Care," *Journal of Family Nursing* 15, no. 3 (Sage Publications, 2009): 295-317.

[188] Recent studies reveal that in the month after the hospitalization, "one in five patients will experience some adverse health event that is so serious that they will require another hospitalization." And many more will need to be seen in the ER or admitted and placed in an observation unit. Dr. Harlan Krumholz is a professor of cardiology, epidemiology, and public health at the Yale University School of Medicine and director of the Yale-New Haven Hospital Center for Outcomes Research and Evaluation.

Harlan Krumholz, "Could Being in the Hospital Make You Sick," *Forbes* (2013): accessed August 9, 2014, http://www.forbes.com/sites/harlankrumholz/2013/01/15/could-being-in-the-hospital-make-you-sick/.

[189] Harvard Medical School, "When Patients Suddenly Become Confused," *Harvard Women's Health Watch* (2011), accessed July 31, 2014, http://www.health.harvard.edu/staying-healthy/when-patients-suddenly-become-confused.

[190] Harlan Krumholz, "Could Being in the Hospital Make You Sick?" *Forbes* (2013), accessed August 9, 2014, http://www.forbes.com/sites/harlankrumholz/2013/01/15/could-being-in-the-hospital-make-you-sick/.

[191] William Silvester, "A Good Death," *The Age* (2011), accessed February 12, 2014, http://www.theage.com.au/victoria/a-good-death-20110319-1c1d8.html.

[192] These authors say, "… medical liability system costs, including defensive medicine, are estimated to be $55.6 billion in 2008 dollars, or 2.4% of the total healthcare spending." Defensive medicine is when doctors order tests and procedures or avoid high-risk patients or procedures to reduce their exposure to malpractice liability. For example, defensive medicine is when CPR is performed on a patient who has a "Do Not Resuscitate" tattoo on his chest. This is what happens in the ER and in ICU if a patient arrives with no healthcare decision maker and no paperwork which says what that person wants or does not want.

Amitabh Chandra et al., "National Costs of the Medical Liability System," *National Institutes of Health Aff (Milwood)* (2010): vol. 29(9), 1569-1577, accessed July 31, 2015, doi. 10.1377/hlthaff.2009.0807.

193   Dr. Manner says that discerning how much defensive medicine is going on is difficult and requires asking the doctors directly. He reports, "Recently, however, a number of authors have identified hard data for the prevalence of defensive medicine. A survey of 300 physicians, 100 nurses, and 100 hospital administrators found that more than 76% of the physicians responded that malpractice litigation had hurt their ability to provide quality care to patients. Because of their fear of the excesses of the litigation system:

- 79% said they had ordered more tests than they would have based only on professional judgment of what was medically needed, and 91% had noticed other physicians ordering more tests
- 74% had referred patients to specialists more often than they believed was medically necessary
- 51% had recommended invasive procedures such as biopsies to confirm diagnoses more often than they believed were medically necessary
- 41% said they had prescribed more medications, such as antibiotics, than they would have based only on their professional judgment, and 73% had noticed other doctors prescribing medications similarly

A large majority of nurses (66%) and hospital administrators (84%) who participated in the survey reported that unnecessary or excessive care was provided due to fear of litigation."

Paul A. Manner, "Practicing Defense Medicine—Not Good for Patients of Physicians," *American Academy of Orthopaedic Surgeons* (2007), accessed July 10, 2014, http://www.aaos.org/news/bulletin/janfeb07/clinical2.asp.

194 Dr. Pat Gary, interview with the author, New Orleans, LA, July 2, 2014.

195 "25 Million Older Americans Have Experienced Unwanted or Excessive Medical Treatment, Survey Suggests," *Compassion and Choices* (2014), accessed August 2, 2014, http://www.compassionandchoices.org/2014/07/29/25-million-older-americans-have-experienced-unwanted-or-excessive-medical-treatment-survey-suggests/.

196   This research shows that, "Physicians have difficulty predicting life expectancy...." I have learned that most physicians want to be honest and because every human being is unique, they honestly can't predict how a person will respond to a treatment.

Lynn Ackerson et al., "Barriers to Hospice Care and Referrals," *Journal of Palliative Medicine* 7, no. 3 (2004): 411-418, accessed July 31, 2015, doi:10.1089/1096621041349518.

197 Dr. Charles von Gunten, interview with the author, San Diego Harbor Hilton and Convention Center, San Diego, CA, March 14, 2014.

198 William Silvester, "A Good Death," *The Age Victoria* (2011), accessed April 29, 2014, http://www.theage.com.au/victoriaa/a-good-death-20110319-1c1d8.html.

199   Remember that Nancy Cruzan was only thirty-three years old and in a persistent vegetative state due to a car accident which took place in 1983. A feeding tube was inserted and by 1986 her parents could see that she was not improving and asked that the tube be removed. The hospital refused to do this without a court order so this case entered the Missouri legal system. When the courts in Missouri Supreme Court sided with the hospital, the case went to the U.S. Supreme Court and by 5-4 vote the court said we each have the right to refuse unwanted medical care—if we are competent. For patients who can no longer speak for themselves and who have not given another person durable power of attorney, (durable power of attorney, healthcare proxy, healthcare surrogate, healthcare decision maker are all the same) modern medicine is faced with a terrible dilemma.

K.A. Koch, "Patient Self-Determination Act," *The Journal of the Florida Medical Association* 79, no. 4 (1992): 240-243.

[200] Jay Katz, "The Nuremburg Code and the Nuremburg Trial, a Reappraisal," *The Journal of American Medical Association* 276, no. 20 (1996): 1662-1666.

[201]   The Nuremberg Trials revealed some medical horrors of Hitler's war. Just one dimension of Hilter's plan was his fascination with what doctors could learn from performing experiments.

United States Holocaust Memorial Museum, "Nazi Medical Experiments – ID Card," *Collections Highlights,* accessed July 28, 2014, http://www.ushmm.org/wlc/en/media_oi.php?ModuleID=10005168&MediaId=2643.

[202] "Law for Older Americans: Health Care Advance Directives," *American Bar Association: Division for Public Information,* accessed August 19, 2014, http://www.americanbar.org/groups/public_education/resources/law_issues_for_consumers/healthcare_directives.html.

[203] E. Chaitin et al., "Physician – Patient Relationship in the Intensive Care Unit: Erosion of the Sacred Trust?" *Critical Care Medicine* 31, no. 5 (2003): S367-S372, S368.

[204] Dr. Joan Harrold, telephone interview with the author, July 18, 2014.

[205] Dr. Elizabeth Chaitin, telephone interview with the author, October 31, 2014.

[206] "Reflections on End-of-Life Care," *California Health Care Foundation* (2012), accessed July 31, 2015, http://www.chcf.org/media/press-releases/2012/end-of-life-care.

[207]   Pam Malloy is the director of the American Association of Colleges of Nursing's ELNEC Project. The End-of-Life Nursing Education project (ELNEC) is a national education initiative to improve palliative care. The project provides train-the-trainer curriculum so that graduates can take what they have learned into their own care settings. I attended the training in Atlanta where the 20,000th graduate was recognized! The program has grown with funding from The Robert Wood Johnson Foundation, Open Society, National Cancer Institutes, Aetna, Archstone, Oncology Nursing, and California HealthCare Foundations, Cambia Health Foundations, Milbank Foundation for Rehabilitation, and the Department of Veteran Affairs.

Pam Malloy, interview with the author, San Diego Convention Center, San Diego, CA, March 13, 2014.

[208]   Dr. Lerner's newest book, *The Good Doctor, A Father, A Son and the Evolution of Medical Ethics,* is the reason I asked him for an interview. His book explores how doctors have changed over the years when it comes to discussing conditions with their patients. Dr. Lerner's father was a paternalistic physician who in some cases made decisions without consulting the patient or family members. While there was a time when the young Dr. Lerner found his father's style old-fashioned, today the young doctor sees the value a physician brings to a patient and their families when they are willing to take the lead. The young Dr. Lerner told me, "Giving advice and counsel is an important part of my work as a physician." Dr. Lerner is a professor at the New York University Langone School of Medicine where he also practices internal medicine.

Dr. Barron H. Lerner, telephone interview with the author, July 19, 2014.

[209]   Surgeon, Dr. Atul Gawande in his book, *Being Mortal,* writes about going with his mother and father, who are also physicians, to hear the recommendations an oncologist made for the senior Dr. Gawande. The author writes, "She laid out eight or nine chemotherapy options in about ten minutes. Average number of syllables per drug: 4.1. It was dizzying. He could take bevacizumab, carboplatin, temozolomide, thalidomide, vincristine,

vinblastine or some other options I missed in my notes....There were too many options, too many risks and benefits to consider with every possible path...."

Atul Gawande, *Being Mortal* (New York: Penguin 2014), 217-218.

[210] Sharon R. Kaufman, *And a Time to Die: How American Hospitals Shape the End of Life* (Chicago: University of Chicago Press, 2005), 147-148.

[211] Dr. Elizabeth Chaitin, phone interview with the author, October 31, 2014.

[212] Dr. Eric Roeland et al., "When Open-Ended Questions Don't Work: The Role of Palliative Paternalism in Difficult Medical Decisions," *Journal of Palliative Medicine* 14, no. 4 (2014): 415-420.

[213] Dr. Chaitin suggests that we "enter into our illness the way we buy a car. Read up on it and don't depend upon professionals. Do you want information on a car from a car salesman or do you go to Consumer Report?"

Dr. Elizabeth Chaitin, telephone interview with the author, October 31, 2014.

[214] Carl. E. Schneider, *The Practice of Autonomy, Patient, Doctors, and Medical Decisions* (New York: Oxford University Press, 1998), 41.

[215] Thomas H. Murray and Bruce Jennings, "The Quest to Reform End of Life Care: Rethinking Assumptions and Setting New Directions," *Hastings Center Report* 35, no. 6 (2005): s52-s57.

[216] Bernard Lo and Robert Steinbrook, "Beyond the Cruzan Case: The U.S. Supreme Court and Medical Practice," *Annals of Internal Medicine* 114 (1991): 895-901.

[217] Atul Gawande, *Better: A Surgeon's Notes on Performance* (New York: Picador, 2007), 250.

[218] Mr. Sabatino writes, "Historically, state law did not identify who, in the absence of an appointed agent or guardian, was authorized to make end-of-life care decisions for persons lacking decisional capacity. Default surrogate consent or family consent laws provide an answer to that question. These exist today in forty-four states and the District of Columbia, although they vary significantly in breadth and depth and legislative origin. Some apply only to particular decisions such as resuscitation or medical research consent. All create a list of permissible surrogates, usually starting with spouse and a next-of-kin priority list. Some limit surrogates to fairly close relatives. Iowa, for example, authorizes one's spouse, followed by an adult child, a parent, and an adult sibling. Others extend this list to any adult relative, with no limitation of degree. A growing number of states, nearly half today, include 'close friend' or its equivalent in the list of permissible surrogates, though usually at or near the end of the order of priority. Arizona, in addition, includes the 'patient's domestic partner' as an authorized surrogate for some health decisions."

Charles P. Sabatino, "The Evolution of Health Care Advance Planning Law and Policy," *The Milbank Quarterly* published by Wiley, 88:2, 211-239.

[219] Dr. Mitchell is a palliative care physician for Kaiser working in the Los Angeles area. He told us that at any one time he is dealing with about one hundred dying patients and over his career has watched families struggle over trying to imagine how a loved one would want to die.

Dr. Michael Mitchell, "The Hospice and Palliative Care Physician," lecture at The USC Graduate School of Gerontology, Los Angeles, CA, September 25, 2014.

[220] David Blair, "How Ariel Sharon Was Kept Alive for Eight Years," *The Telegraph* (2014), accessed July 31, 2015, http://www.telegraph.co.uk/news/worldnews/middleeast/israel/10547657/How-Ariel-Sharon-was-kept-alive-for-eight-years.html.

221 Jeremy Laurance, "Ariel Sharon Dead: How Israel's 'Sleeping Giant' Was Kept in a Coma for Eight Years," *The Independent* (2014), accessed July 31, 2015, http://www.independent.co.uk/news/world/middle-east/ariel-sharon-dead-how-israels-sleeping-giant-was-kept-in-a-coma-for-eight-years-9053476.html.

222 Ido Efrati writing on January 4, 2014 for The Jewish Daily Forward "'Two things make Sharon's case unique,' says Prof. Avinoam Reches, head of the office for medical ethics at the Israel Medical Association. 'There are many patients, surviving through a similar situation within Israel's [hospitals]. That said, Sharon is no run-of-the-mill patient, he is in this respect a VIP. We know that [as per treatment afforded], such cases often see deviations from the norm. There exists a system-wide wish to go the extra mile, out of a fear that perhaps not enough has been done, out of a worry that the system is being looked at with a magnifying glass, so to say. These cases tend to bring up special difficulties. Since May of 2006, Sharon has been hospitalized in a long-term care unit within Sheba Medical Center. The department is equipped with ten patient rooms, most of which are occupied by two patients. The ex-PM is provided with a private room and a full-time nurse to watch over him. The expense of his hospitalization, which also demands the employment of round-the-clock security guards, comes up to some 1.6 million shekels a year ($456,000)...According to Reches, 'The dilemmas surrounding people in such a state are universal: is he suffering or not? Is the treatment being administered superfluous or not? The cost of one month's hospitalization is very high, and at a certain point one is throwing money away for naught. But still, we as a society have decided to accept the 'cost' of such patients. Doctors are carrying out societal decisions.'"

Ido Efrati, "Ariel Sharon's Treatment Costs Israel $456K a Year—Raising Thorny Questions," *The Jewish Daily Forward* (2014), accessed July 31, 2015, http://forward.com/news/breaking-news/190322/ariel-sharons-treatment-costs-israel-456k-a-year/.

223 Just nine days before he died, Ms. James reports, "Sharon, who is 85 and can breathe on his own, has been in a coma and on a feeding tube since suffering a stroke at the height of his power in 2006." She quotes Dr. James L. Bernat, a professor of neurology at Dartmouth-Hitchock Medican Center in New Hampshire, as saying, "Patients can live in a vegetative state for decades. With adequate nursing care and feeding and hydrating them and treating complications like infections. Young patients can be kept alive for decades, but older patients, such as Sharon, usually don't live as long, even with the best of care. There are cases of people coming out of it, but that usually happens a short time after the brain injury. It's rare to regain awareness after six months. And recovery isn't to normal but a severely disabled state, maybe they gain awareness, but not independence. One might argue it's worse to be aware."

Susan Donaldson James, "Dying Ariel Sharon: Aggressive Care Keeps Him Alive," *ABC News* (2014), accessed July 7, 2014, http://abcnews.go.com/Health/ariel-sharon-aggressive-care-alive/story?id=21399561.

224 Jeremy Laurance, "Ariel Sharon Dead: How Israel's 'Sleeping Giant' Was Kept in a Coma for Eight Years," *The Independent* (2014), accessed July 31, 2015, http://www.independent.co.uk/news/world/middle-east/ariel-sharon-dead-how-israels-sleeping-giant-was-kept-in-a-coma-for-eight-years-9053476.html.

225 Eileen M. Fitzpatrick and Jeanne Fitzpatrick, *A Better Way of Dying, How to Make the Best Choices at the End of Life (Why Your Living Will is Not Enough)* (New York: Penguin Books, 2010), 29.

226   Jean Kutner, MD is a tenured Professor of Medicine in the Divisions of General Internal Medicine (GIM), Geriatric Medicine, and Health Care Policy and Research at the University of Colorado School of Medicine. Dr. Kutner received her MD from the University of California San Francisco in 1991 and completed residency training in internal medicine at UCSF from 1991-1994. Subsequently, she completed a NRSA primary care research fellowship, earning an MSPH degree with honors, and a fellowship in geriatric medicine at UCD. Dr. Kutner conducts research focused on improving symptoms and quality of life for patients with life-limiting illness and their family caregivers. Dr. Kutner developed and directs the Population-based Palliative Care Research Network (PoPCRN) and is Co-Director of the Palliative Care Research Cooperative group (PCRC). She is on the Board of Directors of the American Academy of Hospice and Palliative Medicine and on the Society of General Internal Medicine Council. She is a standing member of the Nursing and Related Clinical Sciences study section for the Center for Scientific Review, NIH. Dr. Kutner started and was the founding Director of the University of Colorado Hospital Palliative Care Consult Service. She continues to attend on this service and cares for internal medicine patients at University Internal Medicine Lowry. At the time of this interview, Dr. Kutner was serving as the president of the American Academy of Hospice and Palliative Medicine and she was serving on the Institute of Medicine's Committee on Approaching Death: Addressing Key End-of-Life Issues.

Professor Jean Kutner, interview with the author, Denver, CO, April 7, 2014.

227 Dr. Carolyn McClanahan, telephone interview with the author, August 5, 2014.

228 Dr. Elizabeth Chaitin, telephone interview with the author, January 6, 2015.

229 Barbara Elliot and David Spoelhof, "Implementing Advance Directives in Office Practice," *The American Family Physician* 85, no. 5 (2012): 461-466.

230 Julia Winchester Buckey, "Factors Affecting Life-Sustaining Treatment Decisions by Health Care Surrogates and Proxies," *Electronic Theses, Treatises, and Dissertations* (2006), Florida State University, DigiNole Commons, Paper 2797, 2.

231 Angela Fagerlin and Carl E. Schneider, "Enough: The Failure of the Living Will," *Hastings Center Report* (2004), 30-42.

232 Barbara Elliot and David Speolhof, "Implementing Advance Directives in Office Practice," *American Family Physician* 85, no. 5 (2012): 461-466.

233 Thomas Prendergast, "Advance Care Planning: Pitfalls, Progress, Promise," *Critical Care Medicine* 29, no. 2 (2001): N34-N39.

234   In the case of veterans, some families may want them to live as long as possible so they (the family) will continue to receive benefits. When Pam Malloy did her final edits on the entire book, she added this comment about families of veterans. For many years, her organization, the American Association of Colleges of Nursing provided end-of-life care training to nurses working in VA hospitals. Social workers have told me stories about cases of children wanting to keep a parent alive so that the parent's social security check keeps coming in the mail. Pam's edits were made during the week of January 26, 2015.

235   At the time of this interview, Dr. Kutner was serving as the president of the American Academy of Hospice and Palliative Medicine and she was serving on the Institute of Medicine's Committee on Approaching Death: Addressing Key End-of-Life Issues. This study shows, "Surrogates experience significant emotional conflict between the desire to act in accordance with their loved one's values and 1) not wanting to feel responsible for a loved one's death, 2) a desire

to pursue any chance of recovery, and 3) the need to preserve family well-being."

Schenker et al., "I Don't Want to Be the One Saying 'We Should Just Let Him Die': Intrapersonal Tensions Experienced by Surrogate Decisions Makers in the ICU," *Journal of General Internal Medicine* 27, no. 12 (2012):1657-65.

Professor Jean Kutner, interview with author, Denver, CO. April 7, 2014.

236   Casey Kasem had grown children by his first wife. Since 1980 he was married to another women who, according to reports, never embraced Mr. Kasem's children. He was diagnosed in 2007 with Parkinson's disease then later that was changed to Lewy body dementia. Andrew and Danielle Mayoras writing for Living Trust Network make the point that Mr. Kasem had competing medical power of attorney documents. They say, "Kasem signed one naming his daughter and her husband, a doctor, to make decisions for him in 2007. Then in 2011, he apparently signed a different one appointing his wife in that role. Both sides have challenged the validity of the other's documents, questioning whether Casey Kasem was competent at the time, or whether he was improperly influenced to sign them." Thus a multi-decade emotional pot was stirred when the daughter disagreed with the wife. The big public brawl over Mr. Kasem's end-of-life care is an example of the problems that can occur when we name close loved ones as our proxy.

What if Mr. Kasem had named his attorney or a young colleague or the son or daughter of his best friend? Writing about Mr. Kasem's case in an interview with CNN.com, elder law attorney Ira Wiesner points out that laws vary by state and if you have not named a specific person, many states have a pecking order for designating a healthcare agent: spouse, children, parents, then siblings. However, some go by different rules; for instance, Wisconsin will not let anyone step in to make decisions if a healthcare agent isn't designated, while West Virginia allows the patient's tending physician to determine who will be the best decision-maker.

Jane Caffrey, "Casey Kasem and a Lesson about End-of-Life Care," CNN.com (2014) accessed October 2, 2015, http://www.cnn.com/2014/06/20/health/casey-kasem-end-of-life-care/.

237 G. Gade et al., "Impact of an Inpatient Palliative Care Team: A Randomized Controlled Trial," *Journal of Palliative Medicine* 11 (2008): 180-190.

238 Dr. Laura Morrison, interview with the author, Philadelphia, PA, February 28, 2015.

239 "For Policymakers," *Center to Advance Palliative Care* (2012), accessed February 15, 2015, http://getpalliativecare.org/resources/policymakers/.

240   Pain is big and palliative teams are experts on pain. One veteran hospice nurse told me, "We can bring relief to most all physical pain but the emotional pain is different. Patients can be suffering with feelings of regret, worried over broken relationships or how some in their lives will get along without them. This is not depression. We are seeing that a person dies the way they have lived. Live angry, then die angry." Judy Foreman author of *A Nation In Pain*, disagrees. She says, "One-third of people in hospice report pain at the last hospice care visit before death." Ms. Foreman basically is saying in her book that physicians don't know much about pain. They don't think about it or work on it which is why I think it is smart to engage palliative teams sooner than later.

Judy Foreman, *A Nation in Pain* (Oxford: Oxford University Press, 2015), 158.

241 Dr. Eric Roeland et al., "When Open-Ended Questions Don't Work: The Role of Palliative Paternalism in Difficult Medical Decisions," *Journal of Palliative Medicine* 14, no. 4 (2014): 415-420.

242   Here the authors explain that today you cannot expect "your doctor" to be part of the decision-making about your

end-of-life care. We no longer have a "sacred trust" bond between one physician, we will be cared for by a "care cooperative." To say that it is hard to die or that dying is complicated may be the understatement of the 21st century. The stick figures at the opening of the book illustrate the dilemma.

E. Chaitin et al., "Physician-Patient Relationship in the Intensive Care Unit: Erosion of the Sacred Trust?" *Critical Care Medicine* 35, no. 4 (2003).

243 Robert M. Sapolsky, *Why Zebras Don't Get Ulcers: An Updated Guide to Stress, Stress-Related Diseases and Coping* (New York: W.H. Freeman and Company, 1988), 16.

244 *The Bible,* Psalms 51:10 King James Bible.

245 Bonnie Malkin, "German Recluse Cornelius Gurlitt to Return Nazi-looted Art," *The Telegraph* (2013), accessed July 31, 2015, http://www.telegraph.co.uk/culture/art/art-news/10725833/German-recluse-Cornelius-Gurlitt-to-return-Nazi-looted-art.html.

246 Alex Shoumatoff, "The Devil and the Art Dealer," *Vanity Fair* (2014), accessed June 2, 2014, http://www.vanityfair.com/news/2014/04/degenerate-art-cornelius-gurlitt-munich-apartment.

247 Lynne H. Nicholas, *The Rape of Europa: The Fate of Europe's Treasures in the Third Reich and the Second World War* (New York: Randomhouse Books, 1995), 4.

248 Alex Shoumatoff, "The Devil and the Art Dealer," *Vanity Fair* (2014), accessed June 2, 2014, http://www.vanityfair.com/news/2014/04/degenerate-art-cornelius-gurlitt-munich-apartment.

249 Bertrand Benoit, "Inside the Deathbed Deal with Cornelius Gurlitt to Return Art Looted by Nazis," *The Wall Street Journal* (2014), accessed May 14, 2014, http://www.wsj.com/articles/SB10001424052702304908304579561840264114668.

250 *The Bible,* I Samuel 18:12 New Living Translation.

251 *The Bible,* Numbers 32:23 New Living Translation.

252 John E. Morley, "The Top 10 Hot Topics in Aging," *Journal of Gerontology: Medical Sciences* 59A, no. 1 (2004): 24-33.

253 John E. Morley is the Dammert Professor of Gerontology and director of the division of geriatric medicine and acting director of the division of endocrinology at Saint Louis University School of Medicine. He is the coauthor of the book, *The Science of Staying Young* and Editor-in-Chief of the *Journal of American Medical Directors Association.*

Professor John E. Morley, interview with the author, St. Louis, MO, January 26, 2014.

254 Inge M. Nieuwstraten and Eleanor O'Leary, "Unfinished Business in Gestalt Reminiscence Therapy: A Discourse Analytic Study," *Counseling Psychology Quarterly* 12, no. 4 (1999): 385-412.

255 Ira Byock, *The Four Things That Matter Most* (New York: Free Press, 2004), 3.

256 Hans Selye, "Forty Years of Stress Research: Principal Remaining Problems and Misconceptions," *Canadian Medical Association Journal* 115 (1976): 53-55.

257 "Acute vs. Chronic Conditions: MedlinePlus Medical Encyclopedia Image," *US National Library of Medicine* (2014), accessed July 30, 2015, http://www.nlm.nih.gov/medlineplus/ency/imagepages/18126.htm.

258 "Committee on Approaching Death: Addressing Key End-of-Life Issues, Dying in America: Improving Quality and Honoring Individual Preferences Near the End of Life," *National Academies Press* (2014).

259 "Checklist of Activities of Daily Living (ADL)," The WGBH Educational Foundation and The Massachusetts Institute of Technology, accessed July 31, 2015, http://www-tc.pbs.org/wgbh/caringforyourparents/handbook/pdf/cfyp_adl_checklist.pdf.

[260] "Dying in America: Improving Quality and Honoring Individual Preferences Near the End of Life" (2014), The National Academies Press, accessed July 31, 2015, http://garnerhealth.com/wp-content/uploads/2014/02/18748.pdf.

[261] "Advance Directives and Advance Care Planning: Report to Congress," Office of the Assistant Secretary for Planning and Evaluation (2008), accessed July 30, 2015, http://aspe.hhs.gov/basic-report/advance-directives-and-advance-care-planning-report-congress.

[262] Ibid.

[263] Eileen M. Fitzpatrick and Jeanne Fitzpatrick, *A Better Way of Dying: How to Make the Best Choices at the End of Life (Why Your Living Will is Not Enough)* (New York, New York: Penguin Books, 2010), 217.

[264] "Bereavement Coordinator: Job Description, Duties and Requirements." Study.com (2003), accessed July 30, 2015, http://study.com/articles/Bereavement_Coordinator_Job_Description_Duties_and_Requirements.html.

[265] Elizabeth A. Martin, *Concise Medical Dictionary*, (Oxford: Oxford University Press, 2007), 191.

[266] Hans-Christian Deter, "Psychosocial Interventions for Patients with Chronic Disease," *BioPsychoSocial Medicine*, BioMed Central Ltd. (2012), accessed July 30, 2015, http://www.bpsmedicine.com/content/6/1/2.

[267] "Advance Directives and Advance Care Planning: Report to Congress," Office of the Assistant Secretary for Planning and Evaluation (2008), accessed July 30, 2015, http://aspe.hhs.gov/basic-report/advance-directives-and-advance-care-planning-report-congress.

[268] Ibid.

[269] "ACPA Resource Guide To Chronic Pain Medication & Treatment." ACPA.org (2013), accessed July 30, 2015, http://www.theacpa.org/uploads/ACPA_Resource_Guide_2013_Final_011313.pdf.

[270] D.R. Riddle, *Brain Aging: Models, Methods, and Mechanisms* (Boca Raton: CRC Press, 2007), 5-15.

[271] Eileen M. Fitzpatrick and Jeanne Fitzpatrick, *A Better Way of Dying: How to Make the Best Choices at the End of Life (Why Your Living Will is Not Enough)* (New York, New York: Penguin Books, 2010), 40.

[272] Chris Salisbury et al., "Defining Comorbidity: Implications for Understanding Health and Health Services," *Annals of Family Medicine* (2009), accessed July 30, 2015, http://www.ncbi.nlm.nih.gov/pmc/articles/PMC2713155/.

[273] "Advance Directives and Advance Care Planning: Report to Congress," Office of the Assistant Secretary for Planning and Evaluation (2008), accessed July 30, 2015, http://aspe.hhs.gov/basic-report/advance-directives-and-advance-care-planning-report-congress.

[274] Committee on Approaching Death: Addressing Key End-of-Life Issues, "Dying in America: Improving Quality and Honoring Individual Preferences Near the End of Life," *National Academies Press* (2014).

[275] Eileen M. Fitzpatrick and Jeanne Fitzpatrick, *A Better Way of Dying: How to Make the Best Choices at the End of Life (Why Your Living Will is Not Enough)* (New York: Penguin Books, 2010), 20.

[276] Qian-Li Xue, "The Frailty Syndrome: Definition and Natural History," *Clinics in Geriatric Medicine* (2011), accessed July 30, 2015, http://www.ncbi.nlm.nih.gov/pmc/articles/PMC3028599/.

[277] "Advance Directives and Advance Care Planning: Report to Congress," Office of the Assistant Secretary for Planning and Evaluation (2008), accessed July 30, 2015, http://aspe.hhs.gov/basic-report/advance-directives-and-advance-care-planning-report-congress.

278 Eileen M. Fitzpatrick and Jeanne Fitzpatrick, *A Better Way of Dying: How to Make the Best Choices at the End of Life (Why Your Living Will is Not Enough)* (New York: Penguin Books, 2010), 219.

279 "Advance Directives and Advance Care Planning: Report to Congress," Office of the Assistant Secretary for Planning and Evaluation (2008), accessed July 30, 2015, http://aspe.hhs.gov/basic-report/advance-directives-and-advance-care-planning-report-congress.

280 Ibid.

281 Ibid.

282 "Compassion and Support," *End-of-Life and Palliative Care Planning*, (2009), accessed July 30, 2015, http://www.compassionandsupport.org/index.php/for_patients_families/life-sustaining_treatment.

283 Committee on Approaching Death: Addressing Key End-of-Life Issues, "Dying in America: Improving Quality and Honoring Individual Preferences Near the End of Life," National Academies Press, 2014.

284 Robert M. Veatch, *Patient, Heal Thyself: How the New Medicine Puts the Patient in Charge* (Oxford: Oxford University Press, 2009), 71.

285 "Advance Directives and Advance Care Planning: Report to Congress," Office of the Assistant Secretary for Planning and Evaluation (2008), accessed July 30, 2015, http://aspe.hhs.gov/basic-report/advance-directives-and-advance-care-planning-report-congress.

286 Ibid.

287 David Goldhill, *Catastrophic Care: Why Everything We Think We Know About Healthcare is Wrong* (New York: Vintage Books, 2013), 177.

288 Katherine B. Wilson, "Health Care Costs 101: Slow Growth Persists," California Health Care Almanac (2014), accessed July 30, 2015, http://www.chcf.org/publications/2014/07/health-care-costs-101.

289 Evelyne Shuster, "Fifty Years Later: The Significance of the Nuremberg Code," *The New England Journal of Medicine* (1997).

290 "Advance Directives and Advance Care Planning: Report to Congress," Office of the Assistant Secretary for Planning and Evaluation (2008), accessed July 30, 2015, http://aspe.hhs.gov/basic-report/advance-directives-and-advance-care-planning-report-congress.

291 Ibid.

292 Ibid.

293 Kathleen Woodruff, "Preventing Polypharmacy in Older Adults," *American Nurse Today* (2010), accessed July 30, 2015, http://www.medscape.com/viewarticle/732131_1.

294 "Advance Directives and Advance Care Planning: Report to Congress," Office of the Assistant Secretary for Planning and Evaluation (2008), accessed July 30, 2015, http://aspe.hhs.gov/basic-report/advance-directives-and-advance-care-planning-report-congress.

295 Ibid.

296 "2012 Physician Specialty Data Book," Association of American Medical Colleges (2012), accessed July 31, 2015, https://www.aamc.org/download/313228/data/2012physicianspecialtydatabook.pdf.

297 "Total Parenteral Nutrition: MedlinePlus Drug Information." US National Library of Medicine. 2010, accessed July 30, 2015, www.nlm.nih.gov/medline-plus/druginfo/meds/a601166.html.

298 "What Is a Tracheostomy?" John Hopkins Medicine, accessed July 30, 2015, www.hopkinsmedicine.og/tracheostomy/about/what.html.

299 Lloyd Duhaime, "Terminal Condition Definition," Duhaime's Law Dictionary, accessed July 30, 2015, http://www.duhaime.og/LegalDictionay/T/Terminal Condition.aspx.

300 "Advance Directives and Advance Care Planning: Report to Congress," Office of the Assistant Secretary for Planning and Evaluation (2008), accessed July 30, 2015, http://aspe.hhs.gov/basic-report/advance-directives-and-advance-care-planning-report-congress.

301 James M. Stern, JD, phone interview with the author, July 16, 2015.

302 Inge M. Nieuwstraten and Eleanor O'Leary, "Unfinished Business in Gestalt Reminiscence Therapy: A Discourse Analytic Study," *Counseling Psychology Quarterly* 12, no. 4 (1999): 385-412.

303 Atul Gawande, *Complications: A Surgeon's Notes on an Imperfect Science* (New York: Picador, 2002), 7.

304 ABA Commission on Law and Aging, "Conversation Scripts: Getting Past the Resistance," American Bar Association, accessed July 31, 2015, http://www.americanbar.org/content/dam/aba/migrated/aging/toolkit/tool6.authcheckdam.pdf.

305 Joseph J. Gallo et al., "Life-Sustaining Treatments: What Do Physicians Want and Do They Express Their Wishes to Others?" *American Geriatrics Society's JAGS* 51, no. 7 (2003): 968-969.

306 Dan Gorenstein, "How Doctors Die: Showing Others the Way," *The New York Times* (2013) accessed November 20, 2013, http://www.nytimes.com/2013/11/20/your-money/how-doctors-die.html.

307 "My Gift of Grace: A Conversation Game for Living and Dying Well," version 1.0 by 2013 Action Mill LLC.

308 Jeanne and Eileen Fitzpatrick, *A Better Way of Dying: How to Make the Best Choices at the End of Life (Why Your Living Will is Not Enough)* (New York: Penguin, 2010), 206.

ACKNOWLEDGMENTS

From the beginning it has been my physician neighbors and friends who have kept me on the straight and narrow path I set for myself. Dr. Pat Gary, Dr. Ralph Corsetti, Dr. Gretchen Ulfers, Dr. John Cazale, Dr. Ken Kerut, Dr. Jim Florey and Dr. Richard Della Penna were all part of my social life before I started hounding them for help with this book. Not only did all of these very fine and busy physicians give me long interviews, they read big portions of the book. Dr. Gary, Dr. Ulfers and Dr. Florey read every word, corrected my thinking which is another way to say, "Hattie, you can't say that!" and lifted my spirits in our every encounter.

In the pursuit of truth, I learned that nurses will be key to my getting what I want when I am frail or seriously ill. Nurses like Susan Rodriquez, Robin Rome, Shirley Timmons, Shelly Barreca, and Deborah Bourgeois gave me interviews and advice. Susan edited my own directive and was part of the workbook focus group that offered edits and comments.

She loaned me books, came to my house and told me stories that changed me. It's just that veteran nurses "have seen it all" and I had only witnessed my mom's death.

Two nurses who are nationally known palliative medicine thought leaders, Pam Malloy and Connie Dahlin, read every word of the book and coached me kindly when I needed them along the way. Connie was the first healthcare professional to agree that a physical workbook would make it easier for her to work with patients and families. She was the first to edit on the workbook and even though her work schedule is heavy, she found time to help me whenever I needed her.

Pam Malloy. How can I even tell you about Pam? How could it be that when I decided I wanted to figure out how to get a good death that my study and research would take me back to a college roommate? Pam is a veteran palliative care nurse who runs a large program today that provides end-of-life care training for nurses all over the world! Not only has Pam read every word and made edits, when she spotted a weakness in my data, she sent me the right data.

When I went looking for the social worker point of view, I found Dr. Elizabeth Chaitin, another thought leader. In her first couple of decades in healthcare while working as an ICU social worker, she went back to school to earn a doctor's degree in medical ethics. She too read every word of the book, made edits and when one physician said, "Hattie this is too long. Stop. You've made your case," it was Dr. Chaitin who figured out what to cut. You'll see in the book that she offered up the clearest direction to you on how to choose your Hattie.

Two of my professors in the USC graduate school of gerontology grounded me in the academic research on aging and death and dying. Dr. Aaron Hagedorn and Dr. Susan Enguidanos piled it on and made my work both harder and easier. Harder because there is so much to say, which then has to be edited down, and easier because their courses organized the vast amounts being said by academics on my topic.

My personal friends, who are physicians have been "on my team" from the beginning but I needed more help from more physicians and I stumbled into the most amazing man in my search. I attended a seminar being offered to palliative care professionals only because I found the session online. I called the person in charge, the chaplain at a local hospital, to ask if I could come and simply sit in the back of the room. He was nice to accommodate me so I showed up about 30 minutes early. I knew some of the names of some of the players in the field here in New Orleans because I was in search of people to interview. After meeting the host of the event, the second person I met was Dr. Jack McNulty. He had a name tag and I said, "You're the famous Dr. McNulty." I had read about him the night before. He said, "Well, I'm not famous but I am Dr. McNulty. Who are you?" I told him I was beginning to write a book about how to get a good death. He took my hands into his hands and said, "I'll help you."

That was the beginning of my love affair with Dr. Jack who has been practicing medicine since 1951. You do the math. I was born in 1950. You have to know, every woman who knows him loves him. That may be saying too much but I have met a dozen who know him and the first thing they say is, "Oh, I love Dr. Jack."

Dr. Jack changed everything about the book. Because of him, the titles changed four times, the focus changed and the content got richer. He introduced me to some of the veteran, nationally known thought leaders in palliative medicine. Because of Dr. Jack I was able to interview Dr. Jean Kutner, Dr. Bob Arnold and Dr. Charles von Gunten. With those well-known physicians as part of my expert team, I was able to secure interviews with any and every physician I pursued. With every physician encounter the book got better. Dr. Kutner edited the workbook and took her studied eye to the most difficult material which is found in the fourth chapter. She gave me many, many edits and comments before it was turned over to other experts. You can say she made me look good to all of the other readers. Dr. Arnold is *the* communications expert in this field so it made sense that he took apart my first draft and in a way told me to start over, which I did. Dr. von Gunten, like Connie Dahlin, encouraged me in my voice as a layperson and my idea that a workbook should be the focus of the book. When I get confused about what I am trying to do, I go back in my mind to when I met Dr. von Gunten when he gave me his golden words of encouragement. He said, "We need a book with your voice. We need the layperson point of view. Physicians and nurses have written but there isn't a book like yours." Dr. Kutner sent me to two of her colleagues, Dr. Daniel Matlock and Dr. Stacy Fisher. They gave me long interviews and Dr. Matlock offered to read anything I sent him and many times I took him up on his gracious invitation.

I found Dr. Joseph Gallo due to the study he works on that you read about in chapter three. The first title of this book was, *Die Like a Doctor*, and this is one of the topics that occupies Dr. Gallo's mind. At first

I asked him for an interview about his research which he gave me. When I finished the third chapter, I asked him to review the section about him and provide any changes. He read the whole chapter and told me he liked what I am trying to accomplish and he would be happy to read the whole book before I send it in to the publisher.

I did not want to stop the book at the technical aspects of getting a gentle death because *living* well is the way to dying well. This is why you find the fifth chapter called, *Live Fully All the Way to the End.* This was actually the book title at one time. Physicians, Dr. Ira Byock, Dr. Daniel Matlock and Dr. John Morley kept me straight on my descriptions of our kardia, and, Dr. Morley provided what only a veteran geriatrician would give me. Next, I had to call in the psychologists! Dr. Linda Fischer and Dr. Lydia Navarro advised on this chapter and added instructions for the workbook associated with this chapter and with the first chapter. Like Pam, I have known Dr. Fischer since college days and when I asked her for help she was quick to the rescue. Dr. Navarro has been my friend since 1997. She has read every word of the book, offered some true stories to help me make my point and I don't know how to say what an honor it is to me to have her in my life.

My best friend from junior high school—we met in 7th grade in 1963—is Marcia Kern and she went on to teach high school English for nearly 40 years. Talk about knowing the person who knows where to put a comma! In my television work, Small Business School, Marcia was a key online editor. She read me and fixed me, over and over and over. For ten years she has put up with my whining about what I should do next with my life and was the first to say, "Write a book." Marcia not only has read every word of the book and offered her edits and comments, she read the many book proposals as I was trying to find a publisher. To read some finished work is one thing but to put up with all the grinding drafts is more than any friend should do but she did it.

Marilyn Bromberg is my writing rock. She is my soul sister. She is thoughtful, accomplished and strong. Marilyn and I have been friends since 1995 and when I decided to write this book she said, "I'll help." Lucky for me, Marilyn is a professional writer. She has saved me from myself many, many times. Like Marcia, she has been on every aspect of the process, has lived with me through all the title changes and has spent hours with these pages. She has worked like a fine jewelry maker cutting and polishing to bring the book into a form that hopefully many will want to read.

Thanks also to the team at Bright Sky Press led by Lucy Chambers. It was her belief in the message of my book, and the wonderful guidance (and patience) of her and her team that has led to the book as you see today. It was my friend, Leah Richardson, another Bright Sky author who sent me to Lucy and I am so grateful for both of these accomplished women.

All along, Bruce Camber, my husband has been cheering me on. Putting him on the same page with these others for some reason just doesn't seem right. He needs his own page but then Dr. Jack says this book is too long. Notwithstanding, Bruce wants you to know that all 308 Endnotes are provocative and need to be read. He even loves the Glossary.

Yes, I have been a driving force but most of the credit for what you have in your hand goes to all of these educated, skilled, hard-working and talented men and women who have given of themselves to make this happen.

TIP: "You do not need a lawyer. However, if you have substantial wealth, children who might be prone to argue, or the potential of some estranged person popping back into your life as you are trying to go in peace, you might want to take what you have written here to a lawyer. Hattie's right that giving out multiple copies of your wishes is a good way to protect yourself and make clear that your single chosen proxy is in charge when you can no longer speak for yourself or if you were to lose decisional capacity."

- JAMES M. STERN, JD[301]

MY WAY WORKBOOK

NEED TO KNOW #1:

Everyone Dies

You are living and dying right now. You can't expect to live forever. Before you go on, please personalize and time stamp your workbook.

My name is _____

Today's date _____ My age is _____

The age I feel is _____ My current occupation is_____

Marital status? _____ My household includes _____

(If you have children) I have _____
children and they are _____ age(s).

How I would rate my health today? (CHECK ANY/ALL THAT APPLY)

☐ I am healthy.

☐ I have a chronic disability such as congestive heart failure, hypertension, diabetes or COPD that is well managed with medication.

☐ I have some difficulties with activities of daily living.

☐ I have a serious disease and I need to get my affairs in order.

☐ If my doctor is correct, I may die soon.

NEED TO DO #1:

Face the inevitability of death and any fears you have about it

There might be three good reasons for you to deny the reality of death.

1. *Maybe you deny truth because you have what is called "unfinished business."*[302]

Fritz Perls would say you have things to say to some of the people in your life.

	Y	N
If you died soon, would a person you have been or are currently angry with know that you let it go and you are no longer angry?	☐	☐
If you died soon, would someone you know you have hurt know that you are sorry?	☐	☐
If you died soon, would the people who are so helpful to you in your life have heard you say to them recently, "Thank you for _____" ?	☐	☐
If you died soon, would the people you love know that you love them? Have you told them you love them in the last few days or weeks?	☐	☐

Many people hold on to their heart beat in order to complete unfinished business.

The time to complete all unfinished business is *daily*. This way when your body does want to quit, your spirit can make an easy transition out, as you will have zero emotional barriers. You will have no unfinished business. Think of going to sleep every night as your rehearsal for death. (It is, you know.) Settle emotional problems daily, and you'll sleep like a baby.

As he was actively dying, my father asked, "What mistakes did I make with you?" When I told him the answer to his question, he said:

> I wanted to do what was best for you and guide you through childhood so that you would become a strong and confident woman. I realize now that I was hard on you and judgmental even to the point of trying to keep certain young people out of your life and out of our home. I was wrong. I should have embraced all of your friends and enjoyed them for their unique qualities. I was wrong and I am sorry for that. I am so proud of the person you have become.

Write a list of people you need to talk with right away! These are people you love, people you want to say I'm sorry to, people you want to thank for everything they have done for you, people who occupy both sweet and sour spots in your heart. You want the sour spots to turn sweet and the sweet spots to get sweeter. Even better than talking to the people on this list, write love letters, thank you notes and even a few, "I'm so sorry" notes.

1. _____

2. _____

3. _____

4. _____

5. _____

6. _____

7. _____

8. _____

9. _____

10. _____

Fritz Perls taught that if you cannot speak to certain people because it would hurt them or because they might hurt you with their response, you should talk to an empty chair. Sit facing the chair as if you are knee to knee and imagine looking into the face of the person, then say what you want to say. If you have a friend or therapist observe you, your relief will be more complete, as observed behavior is more powerful.

2. *You may deny that you are going to die because people depend on you and you have bills to pay. The obligations keep you on a fast track and you simply don't have time to die.*

Make a list of people who depend upon you. This would include children under 18 or physically/mentally disabled and unable to care for themselves, parents, a spouse, employees who work directly for you, students in a class you teach, etc. (Skip this section if this does not apply to you.)

1. _____

2. _____

3. _____

4. _____

5. _____

Do you worry that some of these people will fall apart without you?

Y ☐ N ☐

If you died soon, would you leave financial burdens behind?

Y ☐ N ☐

What steps can you take to be at peace over these concerns?

3. *You may deny that you are going to die because you have places to go and people to see. These are dreams. So go ahead now and take action on the dreams.*

Make a "Bucket List" of things you want to do before you die. **There are two parts: one is the list of things you want to do every day, and the other is the special experience list.**

Things I want to do every day.
1. Be grateful.
2. Be kind.
3. Enjoy friends and family.
4. Notice the beauty around me.
5. Express love.
6. Give and receive forgiveness.
7. _____
8. _____
9. _____
10. _____

I have already had a very full life, and if health permits, I still want to:
1. Travel to_____
2. See _____
3. Learn how to _____
4. _____
5. _____

"Mental health is dedicated to seeing reality at every cost. Denial is what keeps us from emotional growth. It is the deepest problem my clients face as they can not get better if they don't face truth with radical honesty. Even with truth staring them in the face, they can stay in their denial and remain stuck in situations that will eventually cause them to lose their minds or stunt their growth. For a person to die peacefully I would say that a person will need to let go of the mythological fantasy that he/she is not human and that the myth he/she refuses to release is very real." – DR. LYDIA NAVARRO

NEED TO KNOW #2:

Medicine Has Its Limits

"*We look for medicine to be an orderly field of knowledge and procedure. But it is not. It is an imperfect science, an enterprise of constantly changing knowledge, uncertain information, fallible individuals, and at the same time lives on the line. There is science in what we do, yes, but also habit, intuition, and sometimes plain old guessing. The gap between what we know and what we aim for persists. And this gap complicates everything we do.*"[303] – Dr. Atul Gawande

NEED TO DO #2:

Think hard and make hard choices for yourself

No family member, no doctor, no psychologist can do this for you. It's too personal.

The following are several true/false statements designed to help clarify your thinking regarding end-of-life decisions. Read the following statements and check the answer that most agrees with your thinking. You'll notice throughout this workbook that there are statements marked with a +. We'll explain what that means later, but for right now just answer the questions based on your feelings at this time. There is no "right" or "wrong" answer. There are only answers that reflect your opinion/view.

	TRUE	FALSE
I am afraid to die.		
I am afraid of the dying process.		
I am afraid my family will fall apart if I am not here to hold everyone together.		
I am afraid my spouse will not be able to live without me.		
I am afraid I will be dependent on others in the last few years of my life.		
+ In the case of trauma such as a car accident or severe life-threatening medical events such as a stroke or heart attack, I am OK with intubation for a few days if I can walk out of the hospital in the condition I was in OR if there is high certainty that I can return to the condition I was in before the trauma.		
+ I want an incision/cut in my stomach to attach a feeding tube if I can't swallow.		
+ I want an incision/cut in my throat to attach a breathing machine if I cannot breathe on my own.		
+ I understand that it is legal for me to refuse medical treatment.		

The American Bar Association Commission on Law and Aging toolkit helps us think about how we want our end-of-days preparation to go. This exercise is used with permission.[304] All answers marked with a "+" are especially useful to your healthcare proxy (more about that in Chapter 4).

It is important to know that many treatments can keep us alive even when there is no chance that the treatment will reverse or improve our condition. Ask yourself what you would want in each situation described if the treatment would not reverse or improve your condition. We give you these five ways to describe your wishes:

1. Definitely want treatments
2. Probably would want treatments that might keep you alive.
3. Unsure of what you want.
4. Probably would NOT want treatments that might keep you alive.
5. Definitely do NOT want treatments that might keep you alive.

On pages 195 and 196 circle the number that corresponds to your desires.

WHAT IF YOU...	DEFINITELY WANT TREATMENT				DEFINITELY DO NOT WANT TREATMENT
No longer can recognize or interact with family or friends.	1	2	3	4	5

Comment _____

No longer can talk clearly.	1	2	3	4	5

Comment _____

No longer can respond to commands or requests.	1	2	3	4	5

Comment _____

No longer can walk but can get around in a wheel chair.	1	2	3	4	5

Comment _____

Are in severe pain most of the time.	1	2	3	4	5

Comment _____

Are in severe discomfort (such as nausea, diarrhea) most of the time.	1	2	3	4	5

Comment _____

Are on a feeding tube to keep you alive.	1	2	3	4	5

Comment _____

Are on kidney dialysis machine to keep you alive.	1	2	3	4	5

Comment _____

Are on a breathing machine to keep you alive.	1	2	3	4	5

Comment _____

Need someone to care for you 24 hours a day.	1	2	3	4	5

Comment _____

No longer can control your bladder.	1	2	3	4	5

Comment _____

No longer can control your bowels.	1	2	3	4	5

Comment _____

Live in a nursing home permanently.	1	2	3	4	5

Comment _____

Other	1	2	3	4	5

Explain _____

Now, read the following questions and check the box that best reflects your response.

	STOP CURATIVE TREATMENT AND PROVIDE COMFORT CARE/PALLIATIVE CARE TO ALLOW NATURAL DEATH	PROCEED WITH AGGRESSIVE TREATMENTS
What would you tell your doctor to do if you had a disease that is incurable and you will become dependent on others for your care?		
What would you tell your doctor to do if you have a disease with no hope of improvement and you are suffering with severe pain?		

NEED TO KNOW #3:

Doctors do not expect as much from medicine as the rest of us do. Doctors know about and use palliative care. Doctors know what their colleague, Dr. Tracy Balboni says, "Medicine cannot give us what we need for a peaceful death."

NEED TO DO #3:

Think and decide for yourself if you want to allow nature to takes its course.

Joseph Gallo, MD, professor at John Hopkins Bloomberg School of Public Health, and a group of his colleagues collected responses from 765 older physicians to learn how they felt about using life-sustaining treatments for *themselves* under the following scenario:

> *"If you had brain damage or some brain disease that cannot be reversed and makes you unable to recognize people or to speak understandably, but you have no terminal illness, and you live in this condition for a long time, indicate your wishes regarding the use of each of the following medical procedures by placing a check mark in the appropriate column."*[305]

Now, it's your turn. Please check the boxes on the following page that fit your response.

PROCEDURE	YES, I WOULD WANT	NO, I WOULD NOT WANT	UNDECIDED	I WOULD WANT A TRIAL TREATMENT, BUT STOP IF NO CLEAR IMPROVEMENT
Cardiopulmonary resuscitation (CPR)				
Mechanical ventilation				
Intravenous hydration				
Feeding tube (via mouth, trachea or into stomach) to provide nutrition				
Major surgery				
Dialysis				
Chemotherapy for cancer				
Invasive diagnostic testing such as endoscopy (equipment inserted in the body to examine an area)				
Blood or blood products				
Antibiotics				
Pain medications, even if they dull consciousness and indirectly shorten my life				

Specifically regarding CPR, how do you feel about its use vs. allowing natural death? Remember that the older we get, the greater the chance that CPR can lead to complications that can mean we're technically alive—but only by machine. Knowing that, if my heart stops (CHECK ONE):

	I want CPR.
	Do not attempt CPR, allow natural death.
	I will have CPR, if and only if, the doctor thinks I will be as good as I was before my heart stopped.

If your health ever deteriorates due to a serious illness and your doctors believe you will not be able to interact meaningfully with your family, friends or surroundings.

Check which of the following statements best describes what you'd like to tell them.

	I prefer that they stop all life-sustaining treatments and allow natural death to come as gently as possible.
	I would like them to keep trying life-sustaining treatments.

WHAT ABOUT PALLIATIVE CARE?	YES	NO
+ If you are in great pain as you become more ill or more frail, would you want your doctors to bring in a palliative care team which provides pain management, symptom management, plus emotional and spiritual support for you and your family and helps promote quality of life?		

If the following will not bring me back to the life I had before I arrived at a hospital...

1. Do you want to be resuscitated if your heart stops?

Y ☐ N ☐

2. Do you want to be attached to a mechanical breathing machine?

Y ☐ N ☐

3. Do you want antibiotics?

Y ☐ N ☐

4. Do you want hydration with intravenous lines?

Y ☐ N ☐

5. Do you want tube or intravenous feeding if you can't eat on your own?

Y ☐ N ☐

NEED TO KNOW #4:

Your doctor cannot decide alone what to do for you when you can no longer speak for yourself. You cannot depend upon professionals only or family and friends only — you need a circle of care.

NEED TO DO #4:

Choose a person who will speak to doctors for you.

If you only do one thing in this workbook, this is the one thing I hope you do. Before you choose your proxy though, I want you to consider the fact that...

A medicalized life can make you and your family poor financially and emotionally.

"Care at the end of life is expensive and too often has no affect on function, independence, duration or quality of life. Furthermore it can cause more pain and suffering with no chance of improving anything. The fact that costs are insulated makes the technology and ineffective care even more alluring."
– DR. RICHARD DELLA PENNA

My dad was good at facing the truth about money because he never had much of it. He grew up poor and wouldn't tolerate waste in our house. He was a conservationist and today we might call him an environmentalist. At seventy-eight he had cancer, and the chemotherapy was a drag. He could see that it was a short-term fix and he considered the time and money being spent on him to be a bad investment. He announced to us, "Save the healthcare for the grandchildren." He invited hospice in and slipped away peacefully taking time to have some nice conversations.

Patients and families often pay a high price—psychologically and economically—for difficult and unscripted deaths. The Dartmouth Atlas Project, which gathers and analyzes healthcare data, found that 17% of Medicare's $550 billion annual budget is spent on a patients' last six months of life."[306]

Need to Do: **Decide how much your own healthcare costs should impact the healthy friends and family in your circle of care. These are *your* thoughts; not what you believe others would expect you to answer.**

BASED UPON WHAT I KNOW, MY HEALTHCARE COSTS TODAY ARE:	TRUE	FALSE
My healthcare costs are minimal.		
My only healthcare expenses are for insurance premiums and occasional doctor visits.		
I have noticed my health insurance premiums rising as I age.		
I am guessing my health insurance premiums will continue to rise.		
I am ready for the cost to increase.		
I avoid going to the doctor because I can't afford it		
+ I am willing to spend my savings on my healthcare even if it means I will have nothing left to leave my children.		
+ I am willing to leave my children with unpaid medical bills.		
+ Money is not an issue to me if I can add weeks, months or years to my life.		
+ I am willing to spend my savings on my healthcare.		
+ I am willing to be sick from treatments if it means I can live another year or two.		
+ I am willing to live a medicalized life. (This means I am dependent upon drugs, devices, monitoring by doctors, etc.)		
+ I am willing to ask my friends and family to support me in my decision to pursue all treatment options that will require their time and energy.		
It would be easy for me to live in my house even if I was in a wheelchair.		

Check the statement that fits you best:

☐ It's OK with me if keeping me alive requires unlimited resources paid for by insurance (private/Medicaid/Medicare), my own savings/the savings of family, and makes heavy demands on the time and emotions of family and friends.

☐ It's OK with me if keeping me alive requires unlimited resources paid for by insurance (private/Medicaid/Medicare) and my own savings. However, I do not want my care to be a financial or emotional burden on my family. So, when my money runs out, let me go naturally. I realize that this choice means I might have nothing left to leave to my children and grandchildren.

☐ It's OK to keep me alive so long as it's paid for by insurance (private/Medicaid/Medicare). So, when my benefits run out, let me go naturally. That way I can leave any assets to my family.

☐ I am beginning to understand that keeping me alive at all costs (money and the efforts required of so many others) is not what I want for my life. I want to leave gently with people sorry to see me go rather than hoping I will go.

Quantity or Quality?

Given the research provided and how you've answered the previous questions, do you want your doctor and others in your circle of care to be focused on maximizing the length of your life or the quality of your life?[307]

Please circle one:

Quantity
(number of days)

Quality
(the stuff of your day)

Regarding quality, physician and financial planner, Dr. Carolyn McClanahan, has a company called Life Planning Partners. The company tagline is "Financial Health for Life." She requires her clients to complete her checklist called Quality of Life Requirements, and wants you to know that her checklist found on the next page is not a standalone document. Rather it is one to be used in addition to other documents related to your life planning.

If your healthcare providers state you will never regain these functions, you are to be provided care that will keep you comfortable and pain free until you die.

In order to live the life you desire, it is important for you to retain the ability to: (INITIAL ALL THAT APPLY TO YOU)

☐ Share your thoughts through words, gestures, or assistive devices.

☐ Understand what people are saying to you.

☐ Know that you are hungry. You are able to eat and swallow if someone feeds you.

☐ Chew and swallow food. Losing this ability results in the need of a feeding tube.

☐ Take care of your own toileting needs.

☐ Take a bath or shower with or without assistance.

☐ Interact in social settings.

List other functions that are important to you:

_____

_____

_____

_____

_____

_____

Family and friends are important to your care. Just like I was my mother's champion, you will probably need someone like me to speak for you when you cannot speak for yourself. The person you choose is called your durable power of attorney or surrogate or proxy. It is a legal relationship, so it is very important that you choose this person carefully and once they have accepted, communicate (possibly over several or many conversations) what you believe deep in your heart is best for you.

You can change your proxy choice at any time. You simply have to ask for all of your first instructions to be returned to you and provide a second set of instructions.

You *cannot* choose your physician or any person who works for an institution from which you purchase healthcare service from unless that person is your spouse or close relative and the person must be over eighteen years old now.

As you think about the importance of this person in your healthcare decision-making, certain characteristics are desirable.

Think about people you know who...

- Would be willing to speak for you.
- Can separate their personal desires for you from your desires for you.
- Would take some time soon to review with you what you are writing in this document.
- Lives close to you or can travel to you quickly or work via phone, email and text with a physician.
- Is young enough and healthy enough to be around in the future.
- Is someone you trust with your life.
- Can calmly manage any conflicts.
- Can stand up to family members who may not agree with you.
- Can negotiate with physicians to achieve your stated goals and be willing to fire a physician who doesn't listen.
- Can listen to facts presented and make a rational decision.

Write your list of possibilities... (minister, adult children of your friends, nieces, nephews, neighbors, one of your own children— the one who is feisty, outspoken, strong, persistent and maybe even considered obnoxious—a godchild, a cousin, a sibling—much younger one—the spouse of a niece, nephew or your own spouse—if much younger but probably not a good choice)

1. _____

2. _____

3. _____

4. _____

5. _____

6. _____

7. _____

Remember we discussed that it's best to name one person, not a committee. There are plenty of reasons that this person might not be your child or your spouse but at the same time, it is your choice.

+ *The person I choose to speak for me if and when I cannot speak for myself.*

1. _____

+ *If the first person I named is not available, this person will step in.*

2. _____

Please turn to page 213 and add your proxy choices to line one and two. Fill in the rest of the form and before you sign, find a couple of neighbors or friends to witness for you.

FOR MY HEALTHCARE PROXY, FAMILY, FRIENDS AND HEALTHCARE PROVIDERS

Durable Power of Attorney for Healthcare Decisions

Based upon the work you see I have done on the preceding pages, I want you to know that if and when I can no longer speak for myself,

_____

Address: _____

City/State:_____ Phone No:_____

will be in charge of making sure that my wishes are respected. If this person is not available, the alternate proxy/surrogate

is _____

Address: _____

City/State:_____ Phone No:_____

I, _____ being of sound mind, do hereby designate the above to serve as my Attorney-in-Fact, for the purpose of making medical treatment decisions for me (including the withholding or withdrawal of life-sustaining procedures, nutrition, hydration) should I be diagnosed and certified as having an irreversible condition and be comatose, incompetent, or otherwise mentally or physically unable to make such decisions for myself.

My named proxies are strong people who know me well and need only to refer to my answers to the questions in this plan which I have written in my own hand or have dictated to a caregiver.

The key information my proxy needs comes from the sections of these pages that bear this sign: + My answers to these questions constitute my advance directive in case I do not take the time to create a separate document.

I understand the full import of this directive and I am emotionally and mentally competent to make this directive.

My Name (In Print): _____

My Signature:_____ Date: _____

Address: _____

In our joint presence, _____ who is of sound mind and eighteen (18) years of age, or older, voluntarily dated and signed this writing or directed it to be dated and signed for the grantor.

Witness 1 Name: _____

Address: _____

Witness Signature: _____ Date: _____

Witness 2 Name: _____

Address: _____

Witness Signature: _____ Date: _____

Congratulations!

Now that you have completed your MY WAY WORKBOOK, PLEASE MAKE MANY COPIES. Make copies of the MY WAY WORKBOOK for your proxy, spouse, doctors, children, siblings, friends, neighbors and any person in your circle who could argue with your proxy over your wishes. You can retrieve free PDF files of these MY WAY WORKBOOK pages from **IllHaveItMyWay.com**.

There is documented evidence that doctors don't even need to see what you have written if others have heard you speak clearly about your wishes, so sharing your wishes is especially powerful, and talking about them even more so. Be open to answering questions and encourage those close to you to do the same kind of thinking you have just done, documented and shared. Then, go have some fun with the rest of your life!

Write me when you've finished this. I would love to hear from you. You can reach me at Hattie@IllHaveItMyWay.com